RETURN TO ELM CREEK

MORE QUILT PROJECTS INSPIRED *by the* ELM CREEK QUILTS NOVELS

Jennifer Chiaverini

C&T PUBLISHING

Text and Artwork © 2004 Jennifer Chiaverini

Artwork © 2004 C&T Publishing

Publisher: Amy Marson

Editorial Director: Gailen Runge

Editor: Cyndy Lyle Rymer

Technical Editors: Karyn Hoyt Culp, Joyce Engels Lytle, Terry Stroin

Copyeditor/Proofreader: Wordfirm

Cover Designer: Christina Jarumay

Book Designer: Kristen Yenche

Page Layout: Susan H. Hartman

Design Director: Dave Nash

Illustrators: Jennifer Chiaverini, Matt Allen

Production Assistant: Matt Allen

Photography: Sharon Risedorph unless otherwise noted

Published by C&T Publishing, Inc., P.O. Box 1456, Lafayette, California 94549

Front cover: *Elms and Lilacs* by June Pease

Back cover: *Sylvia's Bridal Sampler* machine pieced by Jennifer Chiaverini,
machine quilted by Sue Vollbrecht

Library of Congress Cataloging-in-Publication Data

Chiaverini, Jennifer.

  Return to Elm Creek : more quilt projects inspired by the Elm Creek
quilts novels / Jennifer Chiaverini.

    p. cm.

  Includes bibliographical references and index.

  ISBN 1-57120-269-2 (paper trade)

1. Patchwork—Patterns. 2. Quilting. 3. Patchwork quilts. I. Title.

TT835.C458 2004

746.46'041—dc22

0204002561

Printed in China

10 9 8 7 6 5 4 3 2

DEDICATION

To the Mad City Quilters, the RCTQ quilters, and my loyal readers, especially those who made my family feel so welcome when my book tours brought us to their hometowns.

Acknowledgments

Many thanks to Cyndy Rymer, Denise Roy, and Rebecca Davis for their ongoing, unflagging support of Elm Creek Quilts.

Thank you to my wonderful babysitters, Lisa Cass, Jody Gomez, and Christine Lee. I could not have completed this project without you.

I am very grateful for the gifted, generous quilters who contributed their talents to this book, especially Laura Blanchard, Geraldine Neidenbach, Heather Neidenbach, Sue Hale, June Pease, Sue Vollbrecht, and the many quilters who made blocks for *Sylvia's Bridal Sampler*.

Most of all, I am grateful to my husband, Marty, and my sons, Nicholas and Michael, for their encouragement and understanding during the creation of this book.

TABLE of

CONTENTS

JENNIFER'S BOOK TOUR DIARY

Spring is an important season for Elm Creek Quilts. April 1999 marked the publication of *The Quilter's Apprentice* and the birth of the Elm Creek Quilts series. Every spring since, I have celebrated the release of a new Elm Creek Quilts novel by greeting readers on a promotional book tour. Striking a balance between family commitments and authorial obligations is never simple, but the whirlwind tour of 2003 was even more challenging than usual because I had a brand new baby in tow. If I seemed distracted, exhausted, or giddy from lack of sleep when we met on one of my tour stops that year, you'll understand why once you read these highlights of what was happening behind the scenes.

With Michael, the newest love of my life

Tuesday, April 8

The book tour officially begins in my hometown of Madison, Wisconsin, with my first media appearance, an early morning news program on WKOW-TV. And I do mean early. I am due to arrive at the studio at 5:45 A.M., an hour that would have once been unthinkable. Now, however, thanks to my four-month-old son Michael, I never need a wake-up call.

In the evening, the local Barnes & Noble store mounts my first reading and book signing for *The Quilter's Legacy*. I can always count on community relations coordinator Sherry Klinchner for a good turnout, and she doesn't disappoint. Many members of my guild, the Mad City Quilters, bring quilts for show-and-tell, and Sherry rewards them by entering their names in a drawing for prizes: fabric, quilt blocks, and chocolates! Sherry definitely knows the way to a quilter's heart.

Wednesday, April 9

This morning is off to another early start with an interview at WMTV-TV. My host is Nicole Phillips, a popular Madison news anchor and a fellow quilter, who thrills me by citing my books as her creative inspiration. I wish I could convince the skeptical meteorologist that twenty million quilters in the United States alone can't be wrong!

Michael helps mom lay out Megan's Prizewinner.
Photo by Jennifer Chiaverini

Next, it's on to Madison's University Book Store for an afternoon signing. This time I bring the family and a cake. Many of Marty's coworkers are in attendance (aerospace engineers can't resist cake), and the Mad City Quilters are well represented, too. Baby Michael sleeps through my entire reading, but three-year-old Nicholas has enough energy for both of them and embarks on a mad tear through the store with his daddy in hot pursuit. Before long, they're out of sight but not out of hearing. Fearing charges of creating a public disturbance, I consider bribing the store employees with extra cake.

Thursday, April 10

Tonight I load family and quilts into the car for a road trip to the wonderful Harry Schwartz Booksellers in Brookfield, Wisconsin. Ken Favell and staff have supported my work from the very beginning. I see some familiar faces and meet some contributors to *Gerda's Log Cabin* from the first Elm Creek Quilts pattern book. We make a late start home, and Michael and Nicholas fall asleep in the car. Marty looks at me mournfully and says, "Finally they're sleeping at the same time, and look where we are!" We spend the rest of the drive trying to remember what life was like before children. We conclude it must have been boring or we'd be able to recall more of it. Of course, our memory lapses could be caused by sleep deprivation.

Sunday, April 13

My mom, a high school math teacher, is on spring break, so she joins me, along with Michael, for the Ohio leg of the tour. My publicist, Rebecca Davis, has arranged for us to stay in the Cleveland Renaissance, a lovely downtown hotel with a fabulous five-star restaurant. I indulge in a three-layer chocolate mousse dessert and remind myself to buy Rebecca an extra-nice Christmas present this year.

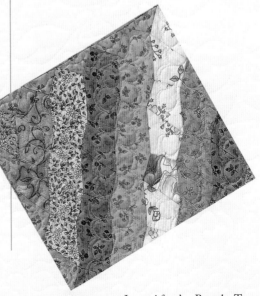

Monday, April 14

Our first full day in Ohio is devoted to media appearances and a book signing at The Learned Owl bookstore in Hudson. My mom happily cares for her grandson while I do interviews and sign books. Occasionally, Michael needs to interrupt the book signing to nurse, but my readers are wonderfully understanding and don't complain about the wait. It occurs to me that I have breast-fed my children in some of the finest bookstores in the country.

Michael and his grandmother, Geraldine Neidenbach.
Photo by Jennifer Chiaverini

Tuesday, April 15

Today we fly to Cincinnati, rent a car, and head north to our next booking, a live interview with WYSO radio. Unfortunately, the directions we downloaded from the Internet are confusing, and even with two maps and my mother's excellent sense of direction, we can't figure out where we made our wrong turn. Michael bursts into sobs as we cruise the streets of a small rural town, scanning the street signs in vain. A glance at the clock reveals that Michael has the right idea. We stop several times for directions, and the friendly residents manage to steer us to a radio station, but when I race inside, breathless, with five minutes to spare, I hear the strains of country music. I realize there's been some mistake even before the sympathetic receptionist tells me that the NPR station I'm looking for is in the next town. Fortunately, she knows the way. We finally arrive, nearly twenty minutes late. The host has been filling time with music. He accepts my apologies far more graciously than I feel I deserve, and after I take a deep breath, we launch into the interview.

Sharon Kelly Roth, events coordinator for Books & Company, greets people while I sign. Photo by Geraldine Neidenbach

It's great to see my uncle, Edward Reichman.
Photo by Geraldine Neidenbach

A good night's sleep (thanks to Michael's cooperation) was first on the schedule for Cincinnati, since media doesn't begin until 10:30 this morning. Just as we are congratulating ourselves on how well we're managing our time, I discover that the hotel clock is fifteen minutes slow, and we're running late. We snap a bewildered Michael into his stroller and race downstairs to the car. Fortunately, it's a short drive over the river to TKR Cablevision in Covington, Kentucky. The two hostesses of the program love quilts and babies, so they insist that I hold Michael on my lap during part of the interview. Being exceedingly proud of my children, I am easy to convince. After the next interview, it's back to the

The evening's book signing takes place at Books & Company in Dayton, a bookstore I like so much I included it in *The Cross-Country Quilters*. My Aunt Ginny and Uncle Eddie, who live in nearby Centerville, are in attendance, as are my cousin Lori and her children. After the book signing, we have a little family reunion in the religion and philosophy section. Michael is a big hit.

During an interview at WRRS-FM in Cincinnati
Photo by Geraldine Neidenbach

hotel to rest, but not before making two important detours: a stroll through the Cincinnati Botanical Gardens and the shoe sale downtown at Lazarus.

The family reunion at Joseph-Beth Booksellers this evening is even bigger than the one in Dayton. My grandparents, Aunt Marilyn, Uncle Mark, Aunt Becki, Uncle Joe, several cousins, and even some of my mom's friends from high school turn out for the event. When members of the Ohio Valley Quilter's Guild introduce themselves as representatives of more than two hundred quilters, I encourage them to bring the whole group along next year.

Thursday, April 17

We fly home to Madison. I have begun referring to my mother and son as my entourage. Now all I need is a stylist and personal chef.

Meeting fans at book signings is always a thrill.
Photo by Martin Chiaverini

Sunday, April 20

On Easter Sunday, my mom returns home to California while Marty, Nicholas, Michael, and I fly to Kansas City for the next leg of the book tour. We encounter turbulence in the skies over Illinois, and Nicholas is not amused. "It's too bumpy!" he shouts toward the cockpit. "Quit joking around!" Mercifully, Michael sleeps through it all.

Monday, April 21

After breakfast, media escort Dick Brown drives Michael and me from one bookstore to another to sign stock. On the way back to the hotel, Dick indulges my passion for history with a fascinating driving tour of some of Kansas City's important landmarks. I wish I could stay longer and collect more material for future stories. Michael and I meet Marty and Nicholas at the Crown Center Plaza for lunch at the Crayola Café. The adjoining shop carries every crayon arts and crafts product imaginable. I pretend we're there only for Nicholas, but I think I have at least as much fun as he does.

At the Crayola Café with Nicholas and Michael
Photo by Martin Chiaverini

With my mom, Geraldine Neidenbach, and Denise Roy, my editor at Simon & Schuster

This morning I change my mind about my entourage. Michael's tummy was upset all night long, and he nursed and spat up at least once every hour. Our early-morning flight to St. Louis leaves us cranky and exhausted, especially me. By the time we arrive, Michael has spat up on every article of clothing I had packed except those I am wearing, and we still have four days before we head for home. I am desperate for a nap before the stock book signings begin. We arrive at the hotel to find that our room is not yet ready. I burst into tears. Michael promptly spits up what appears to be every bit of milk he had swallowed for the past three weeks, drenching my last clean outfit, including my socks.

After a word with our media escort, the hotel manager quickly finds us a room. Michael and I take a much-needed nap while Marty and Nicholas go outside to play Nicholas's favorite game, Throwing Toys into Trees. This time his poor stuffed dog, Rufus, is lofted skyward. The book signing goes well, although one woman confides that more people would have shown up except they have all gone to Paducah.

Although the evening's book signing is sponsored by Rainy Day Books, it actually takes place at the Unity Temple on the Plaza and is billed as a "Girls' Night Out." I hope the girls don't mind that I'm bringing my husband and children along. Nicholas is assigned the job of passing out chocolates to the audience, and he's thrilled to have such an important role. Michael thoughtfully waits until after the book signing to spit up all over my "dress-up" clothes. I decide that I definitely have the sweetest and cutest entourage in publishing.

Wednesday, April 23

Thankfully, we all feel much better by morning. I don my least-sullied ensemble, dress Michael in his last clean onesie, and drive the rental car to Paducah, arriving just in time for my signing at the Museum of the American Quilter's Society (AQS). Afterward we're welcomed to the home of June and Bob Escue, a warm and gracious couple who have hosted us every book tour since 1999. Even as we pull into the driveway, we couldn't feel more at home. Inside, I get Nicholas a snack, nurse Michael, and collapse on the sofa. Marty unpacks and starts doing the laundry without being asked, convincing me once again that I married the right man.

Thursday, April 24

I spend the next day signing books in The Fabric Patch booth in the vendors' area of the AQS show. Shop owner Carolyn Reese welcomes me warmly and alerts me to a line of people waiting at my table. I take my seat, get out my favorite book-signing pen, and get started on the most enjoyable part of the book tour: meeting readers. Any travel woes are instantly erased by their cheerful presence and their thoughtful testimonies of how much the Elm Creek Quilts novels mean to them. When readers urge me to keep writing, I promise them I will.

Friday, April 25

We fly home to Madison just in time for the first farmers' market of the season.

Although the trip to Paducah was over, the book tour was still in full swing. I still had two author appearances in North Carolina to look forward to, as well as my first Quilt Market in Portland, Oregon, where, with Red Rooster Fabrics' Carol DeSousa and Anna Fishkin, I promoted my new fabric line, "Elm Creek Quilts—Sylvia's Collection." In July, Michael and I traveled to Sisters, Oregon, where we met my mother and both of my editors—Denise Roy from Simon & Schuster and Cyndy Rymer from C&T Publishing. We also enjoyed visiting with the wonderful crowds of readers who attended my appearances at the Paulina Springs Book Company during the Sisters Outdoor Quilt Show.

On the beautiful grounds of Camp Sherman, Oregon, before an appearance at the Sisters Outdoor Quilt Show.
Photo by Geraldine Neidenbach

Postscript

As I write, I'm bound for a bookstore appearance in Iowa; then to Houston, Texas, for Fall Quilt Market, and to Ontario, California, for the Road to California show. I hope to see you somewhere along the way—if not this year, remember that for every Elm Creek Quilts novel, there will be another book tour!

Marty, Nicholas, and Michael joined me for a book signing party at the Bear Patch Quilting Company in White Bear Lake, Minnesota. The quilt in the background was made from my first fabric line, "Elm Creek Quilts—Sylvia's Collection."
Photo by Debbie Engh

Until then, I invite you to create your own version of one or more of these quilts, the very same ones that the Elm Creek Quilters made in my novels. Featured here are the original designs of quiltmakers June Pease, who made the stunning *Elms and Lilacs* quilt that graces the cover of this book; Sue Vollbrecht, who created the charming *Wholecloth Crib Quilt;* Sue Hale, who stitched Grace's Friendship block as the heart of *Sylvia's Bridal Sampler* and Laura Blanchard, who made the *Odd Fellow's Chain* quilt as well as *Gerda's Shoo Fly*. My sincere thanks also go out to the generous and talented readers who, in the true spirit of Elm Creek Quilts, contributed blocks to *Sylvia's Bridal Sampler*. The Elm Creek Quilters themselves could not have done any better!

Warm regards,

Jennifer

The QUILTER'S APPRENTICE

In *The Quilter's Apprentice*, Sylvia Compson is devastated by the loss of her husband, James, and brother, Richard, in World War II. Years of rivalry between Sylvia and her sister, Claudia, culminate in Sylvia's shocking discovery that Claudia's husband, Harold Midden, could have rescued the two men but had been unwilling to risk his own life. Overcome by grief, Sylvia leaves Elm Creek Manor and cuts off all contact with her sister, returning only after her sister's death fifty years later.

At first, Sylvia plans to prepare the manor and its contents for sale, but through her growing friendship with young Sarah McClure, she rediscovers her love for her ancestral home. A lingering regret that she has returned too late to reconcile with her sister festers until Sylvia discovers a memorial quilt in the Castle Wall pattern that Claudia had left half finished in the quilt frame. Claudia and Agnes, their brother's widow, had pieced together scraps of James's clothing as a beautiful remembrance for Sylvia, whom they had surely assumed would return to Elm Creek Manor someday. As Sylvia considers the unfinished quilt, she wonders whether they had abandoned the project as the years of her absence stretched into lost hopes for her return.

Claudia and Agnes used scraps of clothing in their quilt, but I used wine, plum, gold, and deep green prints from Nancy Halvorsen's "Harvest Melody" collection from Benartex. The rich, dark autumnal hues capture Sylvia's bittersweet feelings over James's memorial quilt, which she and Agnes complete.

 *Harold Midden*

A native of Waterford, Pennsylvania, Harold Midden might have been Claudia Bergstrom's high school sweetheart, except he was too shy to do more than admire her from a distance. Harold attends Waterford College briefly, but forgoes earning his degree to take a position at Bergstrom Thoroughbreds—all the better to endear himself to Claudia and impress her father. Reserved and taciturn even as a young adult, he is displeased when James Compson marries Sylvia and takes on a more important role in the company—and a higher place in Frederick Bergstrom's esteem. After Richard and James enlist in the army, Harold reluctantly follows suit, motivated not by patriotism but by a sullen unwillingness to allow his brothers-in-law to outshine him. After the war, his relationship with his wife fractures over accusations that Harold allowed Richard and James to perish rather than attempt to rescue them. They do not divorce, however, and continue to live together, albeit estranged, in Elm Creek Manor until Harold's death. Harold's perspective of the wartime tragedy has not been told—or at least Sylvia does not know it.

With a trembling finger [Mrs. Compson] traced one of the quilt pieces, a blue pinstriped diamond. Then she reached out and stroked a central octagon made from tiny red flannel triangles. "See this?" She indicated the blue diamond. "That was from the suit James wore on our wedding day. And this red flannel—why, I spent a good part of my married life threatening to burn this wretched work shirt." She touched a soft, blue-and-yellow square. "This—" With an effort she steadied her voice, but Sarah saw tears spring to her eyes. "This was from my daughter's receiving blanket. My lucky colors, you know, blue and yellow—" She choked up and pressed a hand to her lips. "They were making this for me. They were making me a memorial quilt."

Sarah nodded. A memorial quilt, a quilt made from pieces of a deceased loved one's clothing, made as much to comfort the living as to pay tribute to the dead.

"They must have started it after I left, but—but why?" said Mrs. Compson. "After the way I left them? They must have thought I'd come back one day, but when I didn't—yes, that must be why they didn't finish it."

Excerpted from *The Quilter's Apprentice*
by Jennifer Chiaverini

Finished Size: 78″ x 102″
Block Size: 12″ finished
Number of Blocks: 18

Machine pieced by Jennifer Chiaverini,
machine quilted by Sue Vollbrecht, 2003.

CASTLE WALL

From *The Quilter's Apprentice*

FABRIC REQUIREMENTS

Wine floral: 3⅞ yards (includes outer border and binding)

Plum floral: ¼ yard

Green floral: ¼ yard

Beige floral: ¼ yard

Wine tone-on-tone: ⅝ yard

Plum tone-on-tone: 1 yard (includes inner border)

Green tone-on-tone: ½ yard

Gold tone-on-tone: ⅜ yard

Dark beige tone-on-tone: ½ yard

Wine stripe: ½ yard

Plum stripe: ½ yard

Green stripe: ⅝ yard

Gold stripe: ⅝ yard

Light beige background: 3 yards

Batting: 82″ x 106″

Backing: 7 yards

CUTTING

Make templates from the patterns on page 21.

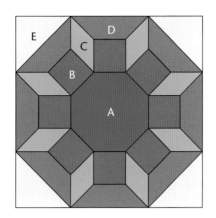

Castle Wall block

Wine floral: Cut 6 A's.

Cut 7 strips 8½″ wide. Sew diagonally end to end (see page 91), and cut 2 borders 8½″ x 108½″.

Cut 5 strips 8½″ wide. Sew diagonally end to end, and cut 2 borders 8½″ x 84½″.

Plum floral: Cut 6 A's.

Green floral: Cut 3 A's.

Beige floral: Cut 3 A's.

Wine tone-on-tone: Cut 4 strips 2⅝″ wide, then cut into 48 squares 2⅝″ x 2⅝″ (B).

Cut 2 strips 2″ wide, layer the strips, and trim one end at a 45° angle. Cut 24 diamonds (C).

Plum tone-on-tone: Cut 4 strips 2⅝″ wide, then cut into 48 squares 2⅝″ x 2⅝″ (B).

Cut 2 strips 2″ wide, layer the strips, and trim one end at a 45° angle. Cut 24 diamonds (C).

Cut 6 strips 1½″ wide. Sew diagonally end to end (see page 91), and cut 2 borders 1½″ x 108½″.

Cut 5 strips 1½″ wide. Sew diagonally end to end, and cut 2 borders 1½″ x 84½″.

Green tone-on-tone: Cut 2 strips 2⅝″ wide, then cut into 24 squares 2⅝″ x 2⅝″ (B).

Cut 2 strips 2″ wide, layer the strips, and trim one end at a 45° angle. Cut 24 diamonds (C).

Gold tone-on-tone: Cut 4 strips 2″ wide, layer the strips, and trim one end at a 45° angle. Cut 48 diamonds (C).

Dark beige tone-on-tone: Cut 2 strips 2⅝″ wide, then cut into 24 squares 2⅝″ x 2⅝″ (B).

Cut 2 strips 2″ wide, layer the strips, and trim one end at a 45° angle. Cut 24 diamonds (C).

Wine stripe: Cut 24 D's with stripe parallel to the grainline arrow.

Plum stripe: Cut 24 D's with stripe parallel to the grainline arrow.

Green stripe: Cut 48 D's with stripe parallel to the grainline arrow.

Gold stripe: Cut 48 D's with stripe parallel to the grainline arrow.

Light beige background: Cut 17 setting squares 12½″ x 12½″.

Cut 4 strips 4⅜″ wide, then cut into 36 squares 4⅜″ x 4⅜″. Cut each square diagonally once to make 72 triangles (E).

BLOCK ASSEMBLY

1. There are 6 different color schemes. To make a block, sew 4 tone-on-tone squares (B) to 4 opposite sides of 1 floral octagon (A).

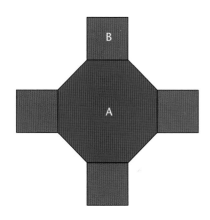

2. Sew 2 tone-on-tone diamonds (C) to opposite sides of 1 tone-on-tone square (B), as shown. Refer to Quilting 101, page 88, for Y-seam construction, and set a stripe trapezoid (D) into the angle. Repeat to make 4 units.

3. Set the B/C/D units, created in Step 2, into the four opposite angles of the A/B unit.

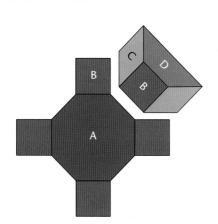

4. Using Y-seam construction, attach 4 stripe trapezoids (D) to the remaining sides of the tone-on-tone squares and gold diamonds.

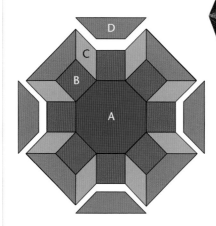

5. Attach 4 light beige background triangles (E) to the green trapezoids to complete the block.

6. Repeat these steps to make 3 identical blocks of each color scheme for a total of 18 blocks, following the chart below.

	Block 1	Block 2	Block 3	Block 4	Block 5	Block 6
Octagon (A)	Plum	Wine	Beige	Wine	Green	Plum
Square (B)	Wine	Green	Plum	Plum	Wine	Beige
Diamond (C)	Gold	Wine	Gold	Green	Beige	Plum
Trapezoid (D)	Green	Plum	Wine	Gold	Green	Gold
Triangle (E)	Light beige	Light beige	Light beige	Light beige	Light beige	Light beige

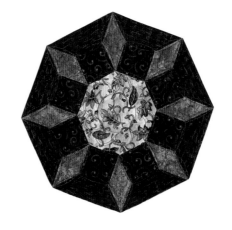

QUILT ASSEMBLY

1. Lay out the Castle Wall blocks and light beige setting squares as shown in the quilt assembly diagram.

2. Sew the blocks into rows. Press the seams of alternate rows in opposite directions or press open.

3. Sew the rows together. Press.

4. Refer to Quilting 101, page 91, for adding mitered borders. Sew 1 plum tone-on-tone 1½″ x 108½″ strip to 1 wine floral 8½″ x 108½″ strip. Sew the borders to the sides of the quilt, with the wine floral strip on the outside, taking care to start and stop ¼″ from the corners of the quilt. Press the seams toward the borders.

5. Sew 1 plum tone-on-tone 1½″ x 84½″ strip to 1 wine floral 8½″ x 84½″ strip. Sew the borders to the top and bottom of the quilt, with the wine floral strip on the outside, taking care to start and stop ¼″ from the corners of the quilt. Press the seams toward the borders.

6. Miter the borders.

7. Refer to Quilting 101, page 92, to layer the quilt top, batting, and backing. Baste. Quilt as desired. Attach a hanging sleeve and bind.

8. Remember what Sylvia would say: Always document your quilt with a label!

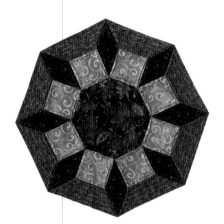

"Why, there's a quilt still on the frame," Mrs. Compson said when the dust had settled. "What on earth?" She bent over the faded cloth and studied the pieces.

Sarah could tell that it was a scrap quilt, and many if not most of the pieces were not typical cotton quilting fabrics. She guessed it was decades old, maybe as much as fifty years. Pieced blocks alternated with solid fabric squares of the same size. The block pattern resembled a star, but not quite … the quilt sagged in the middle as if the mechanism holding it taut and secure had weakened over time. …

"Castle Wall," Mrs. Compson murmured. "Well, if that doesn't just fit. Castle Wall. Safety and security and comfort behind the Castle Wall. Except you have to come back home before home can be your safe castle, your refuge. Of all the choices."

Excerpted from *The Quilter's Apprentice*
by Jennifer Chiaverini

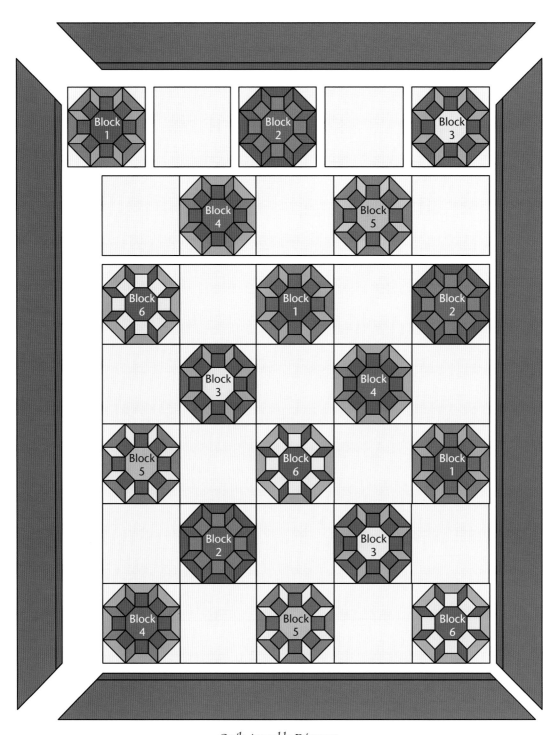

Quilt Assembly Diagram

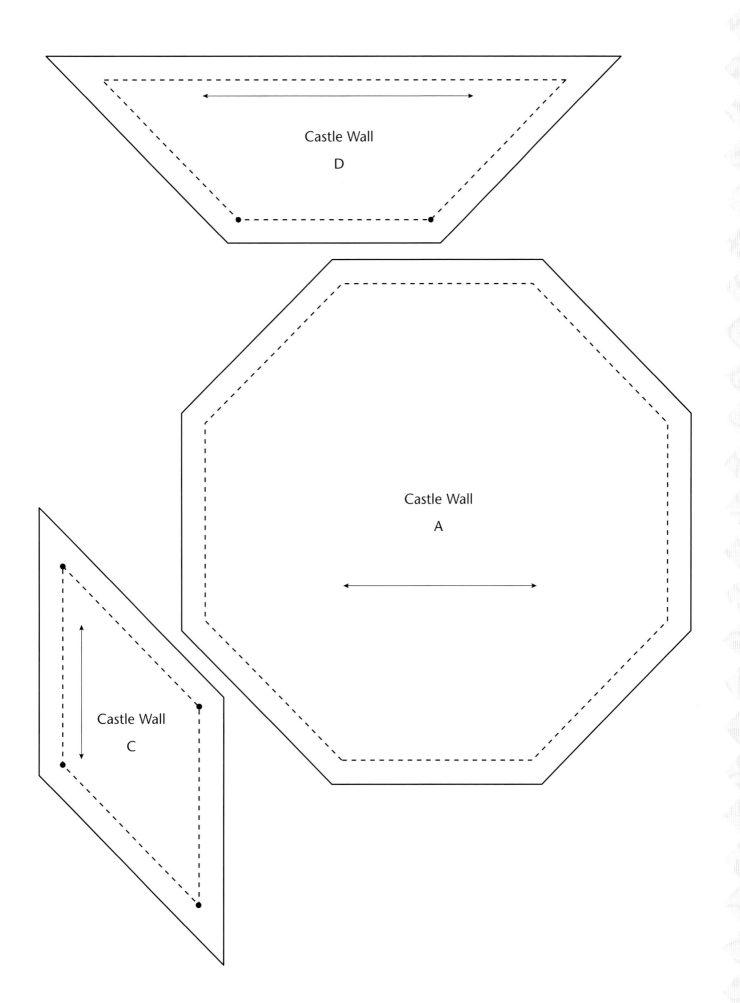

Castle Wall
D

Castle Wall
A

Castle Wall
C

Megan Wagner

A single mother as the *The Cross-Country Quilters* opens, Megan Wagner (formerly Megan Donohue) has since found new love and happiness thanks to the encouragement—some might say meddling—of her friend, Vinnie Burkholder, who was determined to find a suitable sweetheart for her favorite grandson, Adam. After surmounting obstacles presented by an ex-husband, a former fiancée, misunderstandings, and insecurities, Megan and Adam marry and have a baby girl. The couple, their daughter, and Megan's son, Robby, live in the greater Cincinnati area, where Megan is an aerospace engineer and Adam is a high school math teacher.

Grace Daniels

Respected worldwide as a quilt artist and historian, Grace Daniels recently resigned her position as a curator at the De Young Museum in San Francisco to focus on research, consulting, and quilting. Although a diagnosis of multiple sclerosis once threatened the viability of her art, new medications have held the progression of her disease in check, and her new-found hope has brought a remarkable resurgence in her creativity. Grace's quilts have been displayed in museums and galleries across the nation and in several foreign countries. A friend of Sylvia Compson's for more than twenty years, she has resisted Sylvia's persistent invitations to join the permanent faculty of Elm Creek Quilt Camp, citing a reluctance to leave friends, family, and the thriving arts community in the Bay Area.

The Cross-Country Quilters

I wrote *The Cross-Country Quilters*, the third Elm Creek Quilts novel, for all the readers who told me they wished they could visit Elm Creek Manor. This story introduces five new characters (who might be any of my readers), who become fast friends at Elm Creek Quilt Camp and, as later novels show, reunite there every year to renew their friendship. Each woman finds at quilt camp a welcome respite from tumultuous events at home and encouragement from her new friends to resolve certain conflicts in her life. They dub themselves the Cross-Country Quilters to indicate that although they hail from every region of the country, they are united in friendship.

One of the five women, Megan Donohue, won her trip to camp in a *Contemporary Quilting* magazine design contest. *Megan's Prizewinner* is my reproduction of her quilt, which in the novel is described as a one-patch design. I chose the kite pattern as a visual pun, since Megan is an aerospace engineer, and used a Trip Around the World layout as a tribute to the literal and actual journeys she must undertake before she finds solace and love.

Another Cross-Country Quilter, Grace Daniels, has become beloved to many readers and a special favorite of mine, so much so that I could not resist including her in *The Runaway Quilt*, *The Quilter's Legacy*, and *The Master Quilter*. A renowned quilt artist and historian, Grace originally attended quilt camp to find artistic inspiration after a long, frustrating period in which she was unable to create anything new. She first chips away at her "quilter's block" in a photo-transfer workshop where she makes a small wallhanging as a birthday gift for fellow Cross-Country Quilter Vinnie Burkholder. Grace used a photo of Vinnie; however, because fictional characters aren't practical photographic subjects, I used a digital picture of my son, Michael, giving the name of this quilt, *Grace's Gift*, a personal resonance.

Finished Size: 34″ x 35″
Kite Patch Size: 2″ across x 3″ high finished
Number of Kite Patches: 290

Machine pieced by Jennifer Chiaverini, machine quilted by Sue Vollbrecht, 2003.

The "Annabelle" fabrics for this quilt were generously donated by P&B Textiles.

MEGAN'S PRIZEWINNER

From *The Cross-Country Quilters*

FABRIC REQUIREMENTS

Blue tone-on-tone: 1 yard (includes border and binding)

Light green floral: ⅜ yard

Brown vine print: ⅜ yard

Peach floral: ⅜ yard

Purple tone-on-tone: ⅝ yard

Dark green tone-on-tone: ½ yard

Yellow floral: ½ yard

Dark peach tone-on-tone: ½ yard

Batting: 38″ x 39″

Backing: 1⅛ yards

CUTTING

Make templates from the patterns on page 25.

Blue tone-on-tone: Cut 4 A's.

Cut 9 B's. Reverse the template and cut 9 Br's.

Cut 1 strip 3¼″ wide, then cut into 7 squares 3¼″ x 3¼″. Cut squares diagonally twice for 28 triangles. You will only need 27 triangles (C).

Cut 1 square 1⅞″ x 1⅞″, then cut diagonally once for 2 triangles (D).

Cut 1 E. Reverse the template and cut 1 Er.

Cut 1 F. Reverse the template and cut 1 Fr.

Cut 4 strips 2½″ wide for the borders.

Light green floral: Cut 34 A's.

Brown vine print: Cut 34 A's.

Peach floral: Cut 34 A's.

Purple tone-on-tone: Cut 66 A's.

Dark green tone-on-tone: Cut 40 A's.

Yellow floral: Cut 40 A's.

Dark peach tone-on-tone: Cut 38 A's.

QUILT ASSEMBLY

1. Following the quilt assembly diagram, arrange the kite patches (A) on a design wall or a flat surface according to color and orientation (right side up or upside down).

2. Sew the kite patches together into diagonal rows, taking care to sew only from dot to dot and not into the seam allowances. Press seams of adjacent rows in opposite directions.

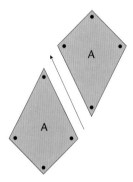

3. Following the quilt assembly diagram, sew triangles B, Br, and C to the ends of the diagonal rows. Sew only from dot to dot and not into the seam allowances.

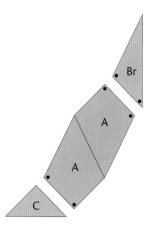

4. Sew the diagonal rows together using the Y-seam construction in Quilting 101, page 88. Press.

---

*W*hen Megan and Robby returned home early in the evening, Megan knew before she leafed through the mail that Keith's child support check would not be there. The day had gone too badly to end on such a high note.

That's why she assumed the envelope from Contemporary Quilting *magazine was a subscription renewal notice and didn't bother opening it until two days later, when she paid her other bills. She would have opened it immediately if she had known that the renewal notice was in fact a letter informing her that her quilt had taken first prize in the magazine's annual design contest, and that she had won a week's vacation at the famous quilting retreat, Elm Creek Manor.*

Excerpted from *The Cross-Country Quilters* by Jennifer Chiaverini

5. Sew triangle E to trapezoid F. Sew triangle Er to trapezoid Fr. Attach to the lower corners of the quilt top.

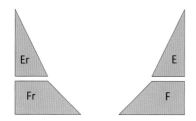

6. Sew triangles D to the top corners of the quilt top.

7. Refer to Quilting 101, page 91, for adding mitered borders. Sew 2 of the blue tone-on-tone borders to the sides of the quilt, taking care to start and stop ¼″ from the corners of the quilt. Press the seams toward the borders.

8. Sew the 2 remaining borders to the top and bottom of the quilt, taking care to start and stop ¼″ from the corners of the quilt. Press the seams toward the borders.

9. Miter the borders.

10. Refer to Quilting 101, page 92, to layer the quilt top, batting, and backing. Baste. Quilt as desired. Attach a hanging sleeve, if desired, and bind with blue tone-on-tone fabric.

11. Remember what Sylvia would say: Always document your quilt with a label!

Quilt Assembly Diagram

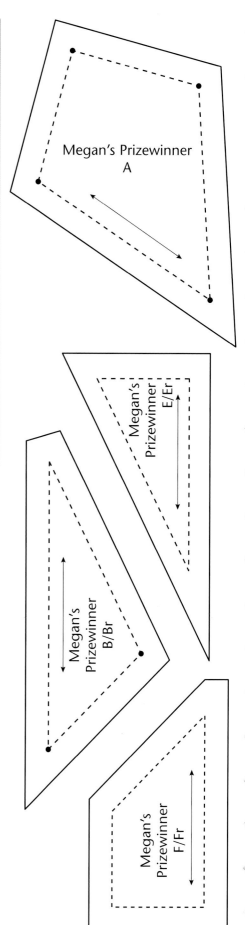

Finished Size: 18″ x 21″
Block Size: 3″ finished
Number of Blocks: 18

Machine pieced and quilted by Jennifer Chiaverini, 2003.

*The "Zachary's Zoo" fabrics for this quilt were generously
donated by Red Rooster Fabrics.*

GRACE'S GIFT

From *The Cross-Country Quilters*

FABRIC REQUIREMENTS

"Printed Treasures" fabric sheet or other pretreated fabric sheet

Turquoise: ¼ yard

Blue: ⅛ yard

Green: ⅜ yard (includes binding)

Yellow: ⅛ yard

Pink: ⅛ yard

White: ½ yard

Multicolored stripe: ⅞ yard

Batting: 22″ x 25″

Backing: ¾ yard

CUTTING

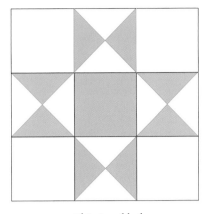

Ohio Star block

Turquoise: Cut 2 rectangles 1″ x 10½″ for portrait borders.

Cut 2 rectangles 1½″ x 9½″ for portrait borders.

Cut 6 squares 2½″ x 2½″.

Cut 3 squares 1½″ x 1½″.

Blue: Cut 8 squares 2½″ x 2½″.

Cut 4 squares 1½″ x 1½″.

Green: Cut 6 squares 2½″ x 2½″.

Cut 3 squares 1½″ x 1½″.

Yellow: Cut 8 squares 2½″ x 2½″.

Cut 4 squares 1½″ x 1½″.

Pink: Cut 8 squares 2½″ x 2½″.

Cut 4 squares 1½″ x 1½″.

White: Cut 36 squares 2½″ x 2½″.

Cut 72 squares 1½″ x 1½″.

Multicolored stripe: Cut 2 strips 2″ x 27½″ on the lengthwise grain for outer side borders.

Cut 2 strips 2″ x 24½″ on the lengthwise grain for outer top and bottom borders.

*A*t show-and-tell on the last day of camp, Grace displayed a small quilt bordered with Ohio Star blocks. In the center was a photo-transfer block of Vinnie sitting in the garden with a quilt on her lap. "Thanks to Summer and Sylvia—in fact, thanks to all of you, for your encouragement—I finally broke through my quilter's block. Happy birthday, Vinnie."

"For me?" Vinnie's eyes shone as she took the quilt. "Why, it's lovely. Ohio Star blocks, and I'm from Ohio!"

"That's why I chose them."

"Oh, my." Vinnie was speechless for a moment as she held the quilt up to admire it, then hugged it to her chest. "I'll treasure it always."

Excerpted from *The Cross-Country Quilters* by Jennifer Chiaverini

BLOCK ASSEMBLY

1. Make 4 quick-pieced quarter-square triangle units for each Ohio Star block.

Note: Because it can be difficult to sew small pieces accurately, you will make the quarter-square triangle units larger than necessary and trim down to the required size.

2. Draw a diagonal line from corner to corner on the wrong side of 1 white 2½″ square.

3. Draw 2 dashed lines ¼″ from either side of the diagonal line.

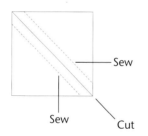

4. Pair 1 colored square with 1 white square, right sides facing. Sew on the dashed lines. Cut on the solid line to make 2 half-square triangle units. Press toward the darker fabric.

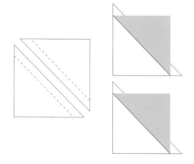

5. On the wrong side of 1 half-square triangle unit, draw a diagonal line from a dark corner to a light corner. Draw 2 dashed lines ¼″ on either side of the diagonal line.

6. Place the 2 half-square triangle units together with right sides facing and with dark triangles facing light triangles. Align edges, abut opposing seams, and pin. Sew on the dashed lines. Cut on the solid line to make 2 quarter-square triangle units.

7. Trim the quarter-square triangle units to 1½″ x 1½″.

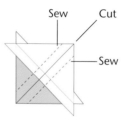

8. Repeat Steps 1–7 to make 2 more 1½″ x 1½″ quarter-square triangle units.

9. Sew the quarter-square triangle units, 4 white 1½″ squares, and 1 colored 1½″ square into rows, as shown. Press seams toward the solid squares. Sew the rows together and press.

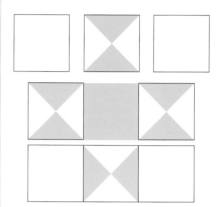

10. Repeat Steps 1–9 to make 3 turquoise blocks, 4 blue blocks, 3 green blocks, 4 yellow blocks, and 4 pink blocks.

QUILT ASSEMBLY

1. Following the manufacturer's instructions, print out your photo on the pretreated fabric sheet. Trim to 8½″ x 10½″.

2. Sew the 2 turquoise 1″ x 10½″ rectangles to the sides of the fabric portrait. Sew the 2 turquoise 1½″ x 9½″ rectangles to the top and bottom. Press. The fabric portrait plus turquoise borders should measure 9½″ x 12½″.

3. Arrange blocks as desired around the fabric portrait. Sew the 4 left blocks into a row and attach to the left side of the fabric portrait. Sew the 4 right blocks into a row and attach to the right side of the fabric portrait. Press.

4. Sew the 5 top blocks into a row and attach to the top of the fabric portrait. Sew the 5 bottom blocks into a row and attach to the bottom of the fabric portrait. Press.

5. Refer to Quilting 101, page 91, for adding mitered borders. Sew 2 multicolored stripe 2″ x 27½″ borders to the sides of the quilt, taking care to start and stop ¼″ from the corners of the quilt. Press the seams toward the borders.

6. Sew 2 multicolored stripe 2″ x 24½″ borders to the top and bottom of the quilt, taking care to start and stop ¼″ from the corners of the quilt. Press the seams toward the borders.

7. Miter the borders.

8. Refer to Quilting 101, page 92, to layer the quilt top, batting, and backing. Baste. Quilt as desired. Attach a hanging sleeve, if desired, and bind.

9. Add a label to the back of your quilt providing the name and birth date of the adorable subject of your fabric portrait.

Quilt Assembly Diagram

The RUNAWAY QUILT

The Runaway Quilt is perhaps best known for delving into the legends of signal quilts along the Underground Railroad, but I believe it is equally beloved by Elm Creek Quilts fans for its exploration of Bergstrom family history. When Sylvia Compson discovers the journal of Gerda Bergstrom, her great-grandfather's sister and one of the founders of the family estate, she confronts surprising and often unsettling truths about her ancestors. One of the more humorous discoveries is that Gerda did not like to quilt; in fact, she despised any form of sewing. Since Sylvia is such an avid quilter, I surmised that she would be astounded to learn she was related to someone so unlike herself. I intended this to foreshadow even more unexpected discoveries—and more startling questions—about her heritage that emerge later in the book.

Gerda, the most reluctant quilter in the Elm Creek Quilts series, learns to quilt only so that she might participate in the political discussions that occur at the quilting bees hosted by the Certain Sewing and Suffrage Faction. Her inattention and impatience result in a first quilt marred by a conspicuous error. Her best friend, Dorothea, laughingly encourages her to pronounce it a Humility block, deliberately included to preserve her quilt from prideful perfection.

For Gerda's Shoo-Fly, quilter Laura Blanchard used fabrics from my second Red Rooster Fabrics line, "Elm Creek Quilts—Gerda's Collection." These prints reproduce designs that would have been popular from the 1850s through the 1890s. These years cover the entire time span of *The Runaway Quilt*, from the Bergstroms' arrival in America to Gerda's twilight years during which she composed her memoir.

Finished Size: 67″ x 81″
Block Size: 6″ finished
Number of Blocks: 80

Machine pieced and machine quilted by Laura Blanchard, 2003.

The "Elm Creek Quilts—Gerda's Collection" fabrics used to make this quilt were generously donated by Red Rooster Fabrics.

GERDA'S SHOO-FLY

From *The Runaway Quilt*

FABRIC REQUIREMENTS

Red floral: 2½ yards (includes outer border and binding)

Assorted blue, red, and brown prints: 14 fat eighths (9″ x 21″), or the equivalent, for a total of 1¾ yards

Cream tone-on-tone: 3½ yards (includes block background, sashing, and inner border)

Batting: 71″ x 85″

Backing: 4¾ yards

CUTTING

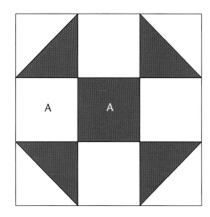

Red floral: Cut on the lengthwise grain of the fabric (parallel to the selvage edge). You will have no seams in your border this way.

Cut 2 strips 4½″ x 73½″.

Cut 2 strips 4½″ x 67½″.

Blue, red, and brown prints: From each fat eighth, cut 6 squares 2½″ x 2½″ (A) and 6 sashing squares 1½″ x 1½″, according to the diagram. From the remainder of each fat eighth, cut 2 rectangles 6½″ x 9½″ (the dark rectangles), which will be used to make half-square triangles.

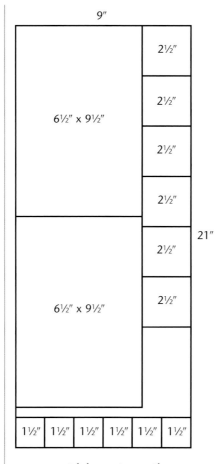

Fat-eighth Cutting Guide

Cream tone-on-tone: Cut 20 strips 2½″ wide, then cut into squares 2½″ x 2½″ for a total of 320 squares (A).

Cut 27 rectangles 6½″ x 9½″. These are the light rectangles.

Cut 6 strips 6½″ wide, then cut into 142 sashing strips 6½″ x 1½″.

Cut 4 strips 2½″ wide. Sew strips together in pairs (see page 91), and cut a 2½″ x 69½″ border from each pair.

Cut 4 strips 2½″ wide. Sew strips together in pairs (see page 91), and cut a 2½″ x 59½″ border from each pair.

BLOCK ASSEMBLY

1. Pair 1 light rectangle with 1 dark rectangle, right sides facing.

2. Using an accurate photocopier, make 27 copies of the triangle square quick-piecing grid on page 35. Securely pin 1 quick-piecing grid to the paired rectangles.

Note: If you prefer, you can reproduce the grid by hand by drawing it on the wrong side of each light rectangle before pairing it with a dark rectangle.

3. Stitching directly through the paper, sew on dashed line 1 in the direction of the arrows. Repeat for dashed line 2.

4. Separate the half-square triangle units by cutting on the solid lines. Remove the quick-piecing grid paper.

5. Press seams toward the dark fabric.

6. Repeat for the remaining light and dark rectangles.

7. Matching the dark fabrics, sew 4 half-square triangle units, 4 light 2½″ squares, and 1 dark 2½″ square into rows. Sew together rows to make the Shoo-Fly block. Press. Make 79 blocks.

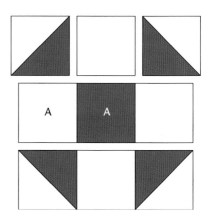

8. Make the Humility block by sewing 4 half-square triangle units, 4 light 2½" squares, and 1 dark 2½" square into rows, with the dark half-square triangle units pointed away from the center square. Sew together rows and press.

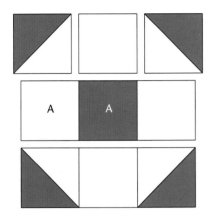

QUILT ASSEMBLY

1. Make the sashing rows by sewing 7 dark 1½" squares alternately with cream tone-on-tone sashing strips. (You will have some squares left over.) Press seams toward the dark squares.

2. Sew the blocks into rows, separating the blocks with cream tone-on-tone sashing strips. Press seams toward the blocks.

3. Sew the rows together. Press.

4. Refer to Quilting 101, page 91, for adding butted borders. Sew the cream tone-on-tone 2½" x 69½" borders to the sides of the quilt. Press the seams toward the borders.

5. Sew the cream tone-on-tone 2½" x 59½" borders to the top and bottom of the quilt. Press the seams toward the borders.

6. Sew the red floral 4½" x 73½" borders to the sides of the quilt. Press the seams toward the borders.

7. Sew the red floral 4½" x 67½" borders to the top and bottom of the quilt. Press the seams toward the borders.

8. Refer to Quilting 101, page 92, to layer the quilt top, batting, and backing. Baste. Quilt as desired. Attach a hanging sleeve and bind.

9. Make Sylvia proud and document your quilt with a label!

To my amazement, Dorothea did not notice the mistake until I prompted her to search for it. Once alerted, her experienced eye found it immediately, and she consoled me with assurances that the quilt was nonetheless lovely. I retorted that it was warm, and it was done, and that was all that truly mattered to me, although it would have been nice to show off my handiwork at the next meeting of the Certain Faction as was customary whenever a member completed a project. Now I considered my quilt unworthy of such a display.

Dorothea told me I must bring it anyway, mistakes and all. "No one needs to know you did not intend to alter the pattern," she added with a gentle smile. "Tell them it is a Humility Block."

I had never heard of such a thing, and so Dorothea explained that some would consider it a sin of pride if one attempted to create something without flaw, for only God can create perfection. Therefore, a quilter might deliberately place an error in her quilt as a sign of her modesty and humbleness.

I found this quite amusing and promised Dorothea that my quilt would be in no danger of achieving perfection even if I had not sewn that particular block incorrectly.

Excerpted from *The Runaway Quilt* by Jennifer Chiaverini

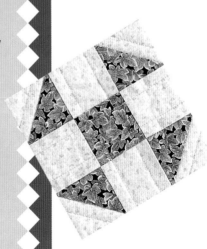

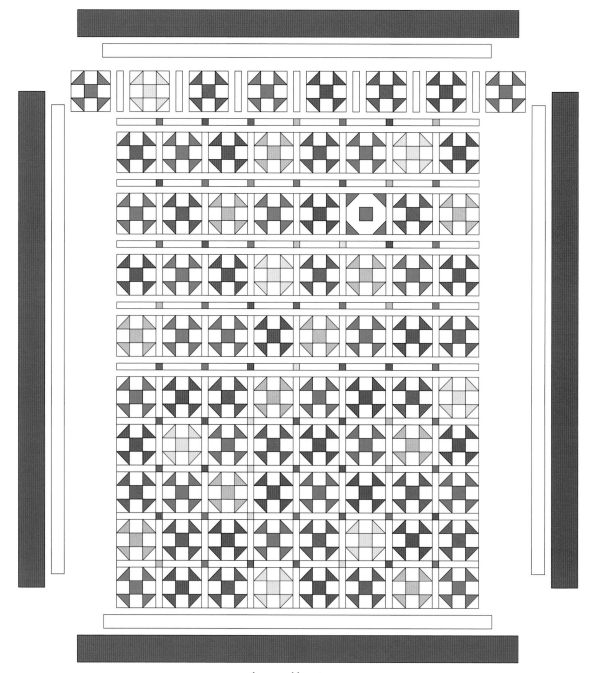

Quilt Assembly Diagram

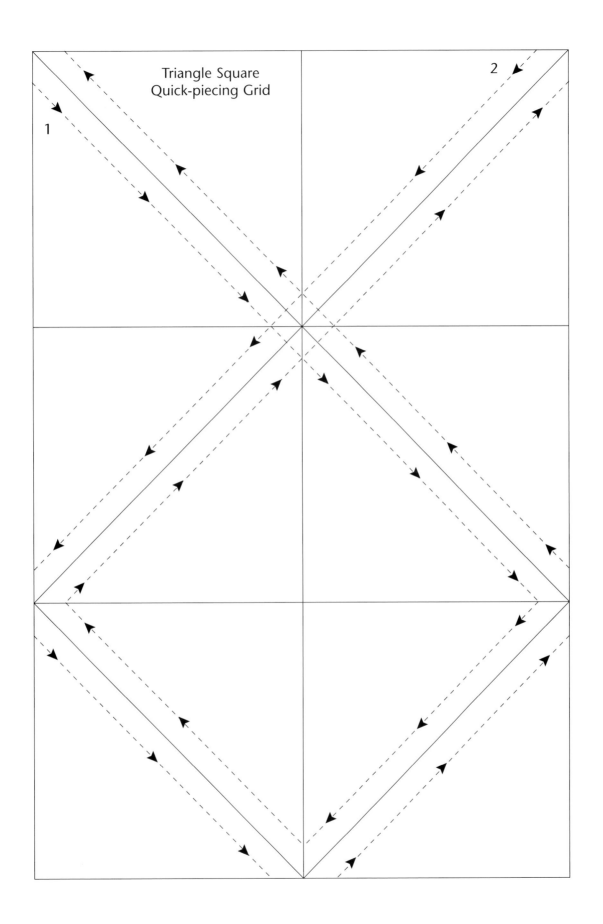

Triangle Square
Quick-piecing Grid

1

2

The QUILTER'S LEGACY

In *The Runaway Quilt*, Sylvia reflects that she knows a great deal more about her father's side of the family than her mother's, an "inevitable consequence of growing up at Elm Creek Manor," the paternal estate. Like Sylvia, I thought I had neglected her maternal heritage long enough, and so I decided to devote a book to Eleanor Lockwood Bergstrom, Sylvia's mother.

The Quilter's Legacy is the story of Sylvia's search for five of her mother's precious heirloom quilts, sold off years before by Sylvia's sister, Claudia. In alternate chapters, Sylvia's investigation is juxtaposed with flashbacks to Eleanor's life. The five quilts Eleanor created represent important occasions in her life, of course, but they also mark significant periods in American history.

The first of Eleanor's quilts, a crazy quilt that I have named *Miss Langley's Lessons*, would have been a popular pattern during that time when American interest in Victorian decor was peaking around the turn of the twentieth century. This pattern's apparently random arrangement of pieces disguises conscious artistic choices, just as Miss Langley, Eleanor's beloved nanny and quilting teacher, has a secret life unknown to the Lockwood family. As one concession to modernity, I embroidered and appliquéd my crazy quilt by machine, but I followed the tradition of using a variety of different fabrics, such as velvets, wools, and silks, just as Eleanor and Miss Langley did.

Sylvia identified the second quilt by its contemporary name, *New York Beauty*, but Eleanor would have known the pattern as "Rocky Mountains" and "Crown of Thorns." In fact, I did not discover this discrepancy until the novel manuscript was in the production stage! Fortunately, I stumbled across this information just in time to write new sections accounting for the differences.

Because Eleanor had intended this quilt to be her sister's wedding gift, the resonance of its traditional names adds deeper nuances to her choice of this particular pattern.

As much as I appreciate brightly colored pieced and appliquéd tops, I have also always admired the skill and artistry involved in wholecloth quilts, so I decided Eleanor would, too. When the time came to design Eleanor's whole-cloth crib quilt, I sought out the expertise of my friend and fellow Mad City Quilter Sue Vollbrecht, who took my description from the pages of *The Quilter's Legacy* and turned it into the beautiful quilt featured here.

Like the *New York Beauty*, *Eleanor's Ocean Waves* quilt also had another name—"The Sick Quilt"—ascribed to it by Eleanor's superstitious mother-in-law, who believed that sleeping beneath the quilt would cure one's illnesses and relieve pain. Eleanor, who chose the pattern to represent the ocean that separated her from her husband serving overseas in World War I, did not share this belief, although she would occasionally pretend to do so to humor her mother-in-law. I updated the *Ocean Waves* quilt especially for quick-piecing enthusiasts and am proud to say it was made by my two favorite quilters: my mother, Geraldine Neidenbach, and my sister, Heather Neidenbach.

I relied upon another talented quiltmaker, June Pease, for the *Elms and Lilacs* quilt, which Sylvia calls her "favorite of all her mother's quilts; indeed, it was quite possibly her favorite out of all the quilts she had ever seen." Eleanor made this quilt as a twentieth anniversary gift for her husband, Frederick, as an expression of all that she loved best about Elm Creek Manor. When I saw how beautifully June translated my vision of Eleanor's masterpiece into reality, I was thrilled, just as I'm certain Eleanor and Sylvia would be.

Frederick Bergstrom

The eldest son of David and Elizabeth Bergstrom, Frederick begins learning the family trade, horse breeding, at an early age. At eleven, he meets his future wife, Eleanor, while traveling with his father on business for Bergstrom Thoroughbreds; eight years later, he helps her escape a hastily arranged, financially motivated marriage by declaring his love—and offering her a ride from her parents' home to the house where the couple will live as man and wife. Stationed overseas as a cavalry officer in World War I, he returns home to devote himself to his wife, children, and the family business, eventually succeeding his aging father as the head of Bergstrom Thoroughbreds.

Finished Size: 38″ x 48″
Block Size: 6″ across x 8″ high finished
Number of Blocks: 41 full diamonds, 20 partial

Machine pieced and embroidered by Jennifer Chiaverini, 2003.

MISS LANGLEY'S LESSONS
(CRAZY QUILT)

From *The Quilter's Legacy*

FABRIC REQUIREMENTS

Black velvet, satin, or other textured fabric: 1⅞ yards (includes border)

Assorted fabrics in a variety of colors and textures: 5 yards total

Muslin: 2 yards

Satin or other fabric for lining: 1½ yards

Decorative thread or embroidery floss

CUTTING

Make templates from patterns on pages 42–43.

Black velvet, satin, or other textured fabric: Cut 2 border strips 4½″ x 53″ on the lengthwise grain (parallel to selvage edges).

Cut 2 strips 4½″ x 42″ on the crosswise grain (from selvage to selvage).

Assorted fabrics in a variety of colors and textures: Cut pieces of varying sizes and shapes as the quilt progresses.

Muslin: Cut 41 A's.

Cut 8 B's.

Cut 8 C's.

Cut 2 D's. Reverse the template and cut 2 Dr's.

Note: Using freezer paper instead of muslin as the foundation is another option. Use a smaller stitch length when piecing. Remember to remove the paper after sewing the quilt top together.

BLOCK ASSEMBLY

1. Cut an irregular 4-, 5-, or 6-sided shape from the assortment of fabric. Place right side up at the approximate center of the muslin foundation.

2. Place a second piece on top of the first, right sides facing. Sew the second piece onto the first using a ¼″ seam allowance.

3. Trim excess fabric from the seam allowance, if necessary. Fold over the second piece and press both pieces flat.

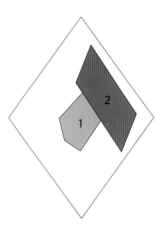

The crazy quilt was the one sign of chaos in Miss Langley's ordered world, the one nod to ornamentation for the sheer pleasure of it in a room dedicated to usefulness and practicality. When Eleanor was ill or downcast, Miss Langley would let her curl up beneath the quilt in the window seat in the conservatory, warmed by the privilege rather than the quilt itself, which in the style of crazy quilts, was pieced of more delicate fabrics than traditional quilts and had no inner layer of batting.

Excerpted from *The Quilter's Legacy*,
by Jennifer Chiaverini

4. Move clockwise to the next side of the center shape and attach a third piece, taking care that it completely covers the edges of the first two pieces. Trim excess fabric from the seam allowance, if necessary. Fold over the third piece and press.

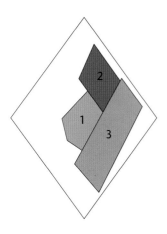

5. Continue adding fabric pieces in a clockwise direction until the entire diamond foundation, including block seam allowance, is covered. Trim outermost fabrics even with the edge of the foundation to complete the block.

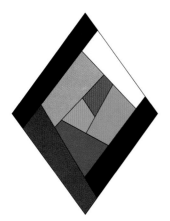

6. In this same manner, make 41 of block A, 8 of block B, 8 of block C, 2 of block D, and 2 of block Dr.

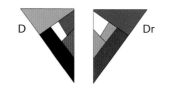

7. Embellish the blocks with embroidery and/or appliqué by hand or machine.

QUILT ASSEMBLY

1. Sew the blocks into diagonal rows. Press the seams of adjacent rows in alternate directions.

2. Sew the rows together. Press.

3. Refer to Quilting 101, page 91, for adding mitered borders. Sew the long borders to the sides of the quilt, taking care to start and stop ¼″ from the corners of the quilt. Press the seams toward the borders.

4. Sew the 2 shorter borders to the top and bottom of the quilt, taking care to start and stop ¼″ from the corners of the quilt. Press the seams toward the borders.

5. Miter the borders.

6. Layer with the satin lining and bind; or, if preferred, place the quilt top and lining together with right sides facing and sew around the edges with a ¼″ seam, leaving a 5″ opening unsewn. Turn the quilt right side out and hand sew the opening closed.

Note: Because crazy quilts were traditionally made for decoration rather than for use as bed quilts, adding batting and quilting or tying the layers is optional.

7. Instead of a label for the back, embroider your name, place of residence, and the date on the front of the quilt in the border.

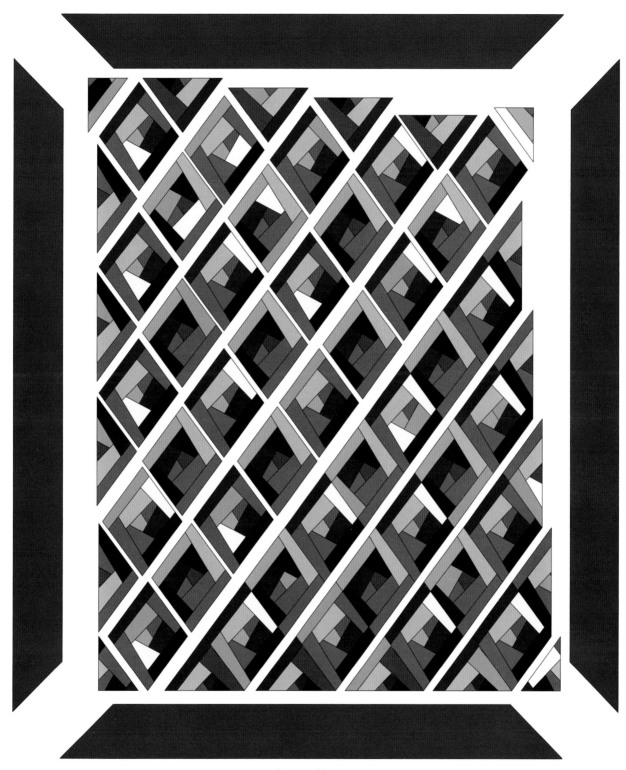

Quilt Assembly Diagram

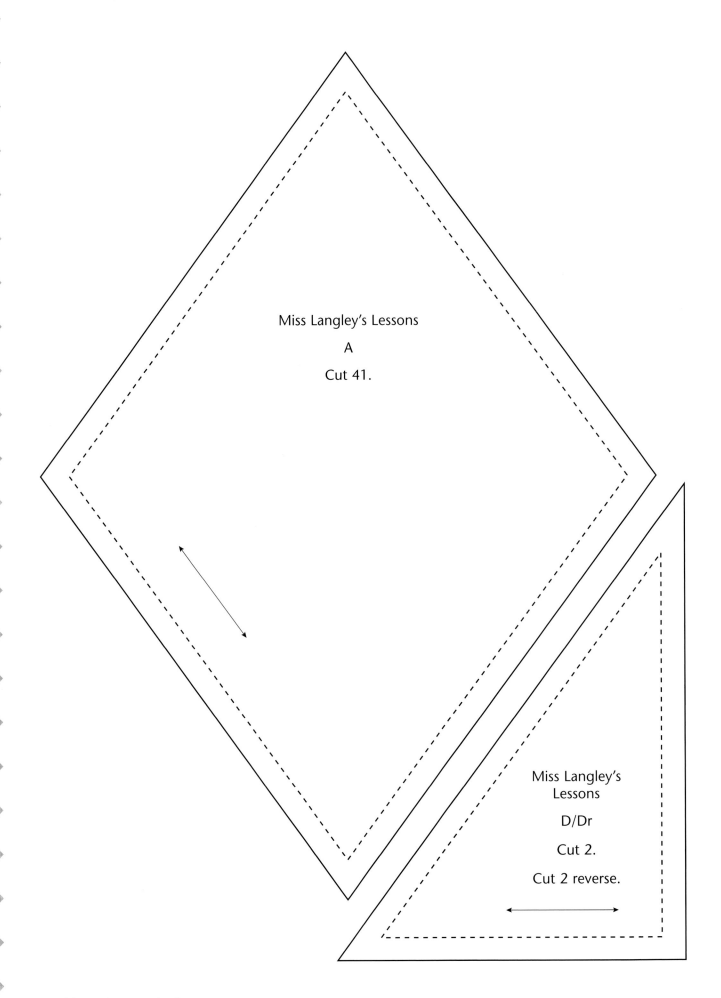

Miss Langley's Lessons

A

Cut 41.

Miss Langley's
Lessons

D/Dr

Cut 2.

Cut 2 reverse.

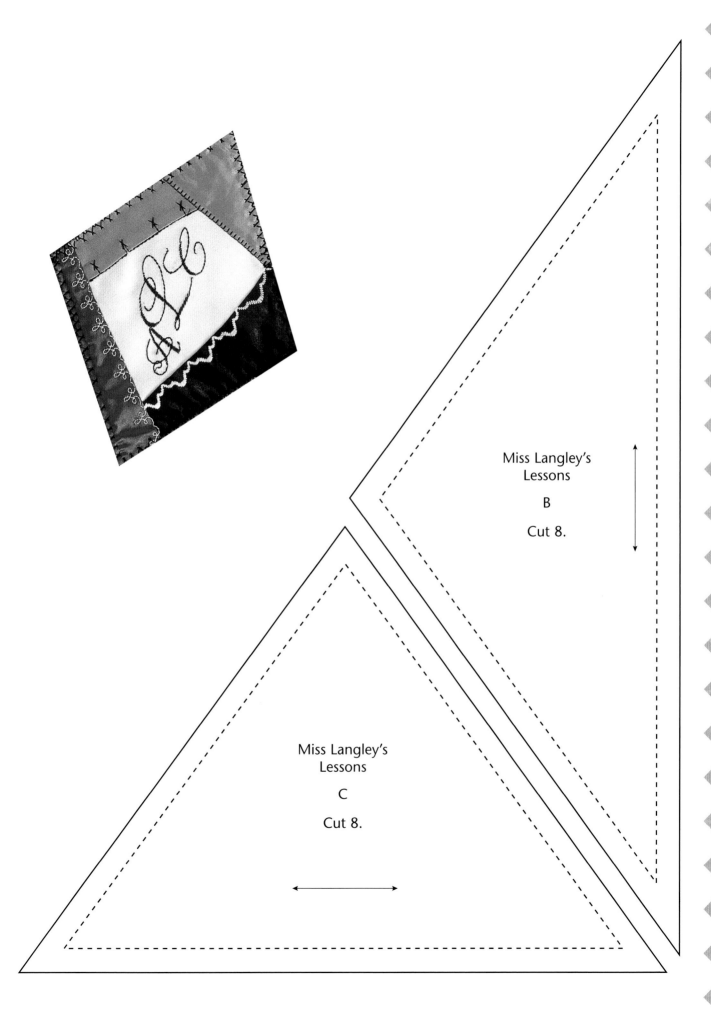

Miss Langley's
Lessons

B

Cut 8.

Miss Langley's
Lessons

C

Cut 8.

Finished Size: 82″ x 113″

Block Size: 8¼″ finished (New York Beauty), 5½″ finished (LeMoyne Star)

Number of Blocks: 32 New York Beauty blocks, 17 LeMoyne Star blocks

Machine pieced by Jennifer Chiaverini, machine quilted by Sue Vollbrecht, 2003.

NEW YORK BEAUTY

From *The Quilter's Legacy*

FABRIC REQUIREMENTS

Assorted black prints: 1½ yards

Assorted burgundy prints: 2¼ yards

Assorted green prints: 7 yards
(includes binding)

Black vine print: 1 yard

White tone-on-tone: 10¾ yards

Burgundy tone-on-tone: 1 yard for
inner border

Batting: 86″ x 117″

Backing: 7¼ yards

CUTTING

*Make templates from patterns A, B, C,
and D on pages 50–51.*

New York Beauty

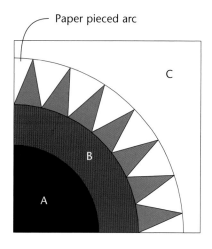

Paper pieced arc

New York Beauty block

Assorted black prints: Cut 38 A's.

Assorted burgundy prints: Cut 38 B's.

Assorted green prints: Cut 2″-wide
strips as needed for paper piecing.

Black vine print: Cut 24 strips 2″ x
17″.

White tone-on-tone: Enlarge the New
York Beauty pattern C on page 51 by
200%. Cut 32 C's.

Cut 2½″-wide strips as needed for
paper piecing.

LeMoyne Star

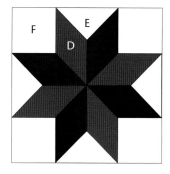

LeMoyne Star block

Assorted black prints: Cut groups of 4
diamonds (D) from the same fabric
for a total of 68.

Assorted burgundy prints: Cut groups
of 4 diamonds (D) from the same
fabric for a total of 68.

White tone-on-tone: Cut 2 strips 3½″
wide, then cut into 17 squares 3½″ x
3½″. Cut the squares diagonally twice
for 68 triangles (E).

Cut 4 strips 2⅛″ wide, then cut into
68 squares 2⅛″ x 2⅛″ (F).

Setting Triangles

White tone-on-tone: Cut 2 squares
32⅜″ x 32⅜″, then cut diagonally
twice to make 6 side setting triangles.
There will be 2 extra triangles.

Cut 2 squares 20⅜″ x 20⅜″, then cut
diagonally once to make 4 corner setting triangles.

Borders

Burgundy tone-on-tone: Cut 6 strips 2½" wide. Sew diagonally end to end (see page 91), and cut 2 borders 2½" x 101½".

Cut 4 strips 2½" wide. Sew strips together in pairs (see page 91), and cut a 2½" x 74½" border from each pair.

Assorted green prints: Cut the remainder into 2½"-wide strips for the pieced borders.

BLOCK ASSEMBLY

New York Beauty

1. Refer to Quilting 101, page 89, for paper-piecing instructions. Make 38 copies of the paper-pieced arc pattern on page 51.

2. Beginning with white and alternating with assorted green fabrics, paper piece 38 New York Beauty arcs.

3. Pair 1 block quarter-circle A with 1 burgundy solid arc B. Pin carefully, clipping and easing the concave arc around the curve of the quarter-circle. Sew. Press toward the burgundy solid arc. Repeat to make 38.

4. Pair 1 foundation paper-pieced arc with 1 A/B unit created in Step 3. Pin carefully, clipping and easing the concave arc around the convex curve. Sew. Press toward the burgundy solid arc. Repeat to make 38.

5. Attach 1 background piece C to 1 of the A/B/arc units created in Step 4. Remove the paper and press toward the pieced arc. Repeat to make 32. Set aside the remaining 6 A/B/arc units.

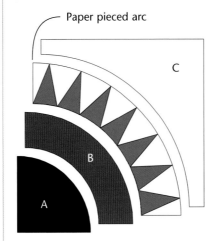

New York Beauty block

LeMoyne Star

1. Refer to Quilting 101, page 88, for Y-seam construction. Sew a black diamond (D) and a burgundy diamond (D) to opposite sides of a white triangle (E). Take care not to sew into the seam allowance. Make 4 D/E/D units.

Make 4.

2. Sew 1 white square (F) to the black diamond, taking care not to sew into the seam allowance.

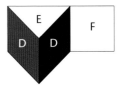

Make 4.

3. Sew together 2 D/D/E/F units, stitching from point to point in the direction of the arrows. Press. Repeat to make a second identical unit.

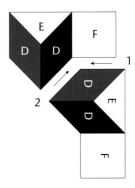

4. Sew the 2 halves together to complete the LeMoyne Star block. Press.

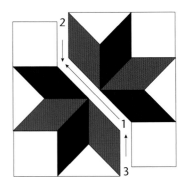

5. Repeat to make 17 blocks.

PIECED SASHING ASSEMBLY

1. Refer to Quilting 101, page 89, for paper-piecing instructions. Make 48 copies of the sashing paper-piecing pattern on page 50. Beginning with white and alternating with assorted green prints, paper piece 48 sashing strips.

2. Join 2 pieced sashing strips together with a black vine print 2″ x 17″ rectangle to make a pieced sashing unit. Make 24.

Make 24.

3. Make 5 sashing rows by alternating LeMoyne Stars with pieced sashing units.

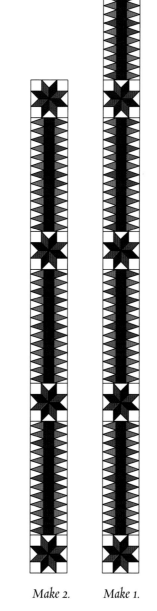

Make 2.　　*Make 2.*　　*Make 1.*

QUILT ASSEMBLY

1. Sew the New York Beauty blocks together in groups of 4, with the black quarter-circles (A) in the corners, to make 4-block units.

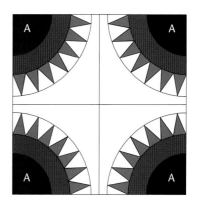

Make 8.

2. Attach 2 pieced sashing units to opposite sides of 6 New York Beauty 4-block units.

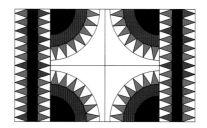

Make 6.

3. Sew 2 of the units created in Step 2 to opposite sides of a New York Beauty 4-block unit. Make a second identical row.

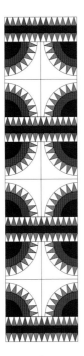

Make 2.

4. Attach 2-star and 4-star sashing to the rows created in Steps 2 and 3.

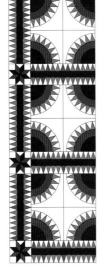

Make 2.   *Make 2.*

5. Appliqué 1 A/B/arc unit in the corner of each setting triangle. Trim the excess fabric beneath. Make 6 New York Beauty setting triangles.

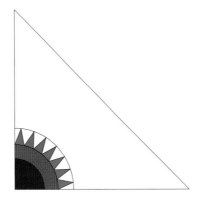

Make 6.

6. Following the quilt assembly diagram, sew the units from Step 4, the New York Beauty setting triangles, and the corner triangles into diagonal rows. Press.

7. Sew rows together. Press. Sew corner triangles on. Press.

8. Refer to Quilting 101, page 91, for adding butted borders. Sew the burgundy tone-on-tone 2½" x 101½" borders to the sides of the quilt. Press the seams toward the borders.

9. Sew the burgundy tone-on-tone 2½" x 74½" borders to the top and bottom of the quilt. Press the seams toward the borders.

10. Sew the 2½"-wide strips from the assorted green fabrics together lengthwise. Press. With a rotary cutter and ruler, cut the strip sets into 4½" sections.

Note: The number of border sections needed depends on the number of green fabric strips sewn together.

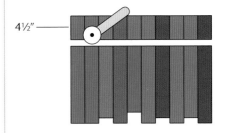

4½"

11. Sew the sections together end to end to make 2 borders 105½" long and 2 borders 82½" long.

Gazing at the quilt that had so long eluded her, Sylvia resolved to gather the precious scraps of her mother's history and piece them together until a pattern emerged, until she understood as well as any daughter could the choices her mother had made. She had no daughter to pass those stories along to, but she had Sarah, and she had Andrew's children, and among them she would surely find one who would listen, so that her mother's memory would endure.

Excerpted from *The Quilter's Legacy*
by Jennifer Chiaverini

12. Sew the longer pieced borders to the sides of the quilt. Sew the shorter pieced borders to the top and bottom. Press toward the burgundy border.

13. Refer to Quilting 101, page 92, to layer the quilt top, batting, and backing. Baste. Quilt as desired. Attach a hanging sleeve, if desired, and bind.

14. Make a label with your name, location, and the date the quilt was completed. Appliqué to the back of the quilt.

Quilt Assembly Diagram

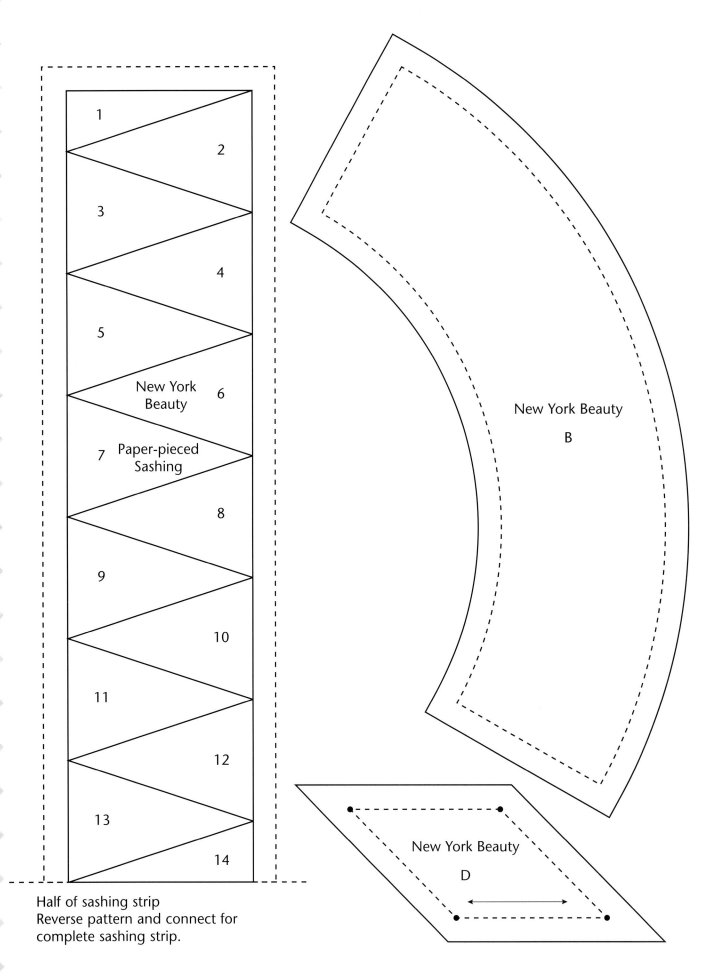

1

2

3

4

5

New York
Beauty   6

7   Paper-pieced
    Sashing

8

9

10

11

12

13

14

Half of sashing strip
Reverse pattern and connect for
complete sashing strip.

New York Beauty

B

New York Beauty

D

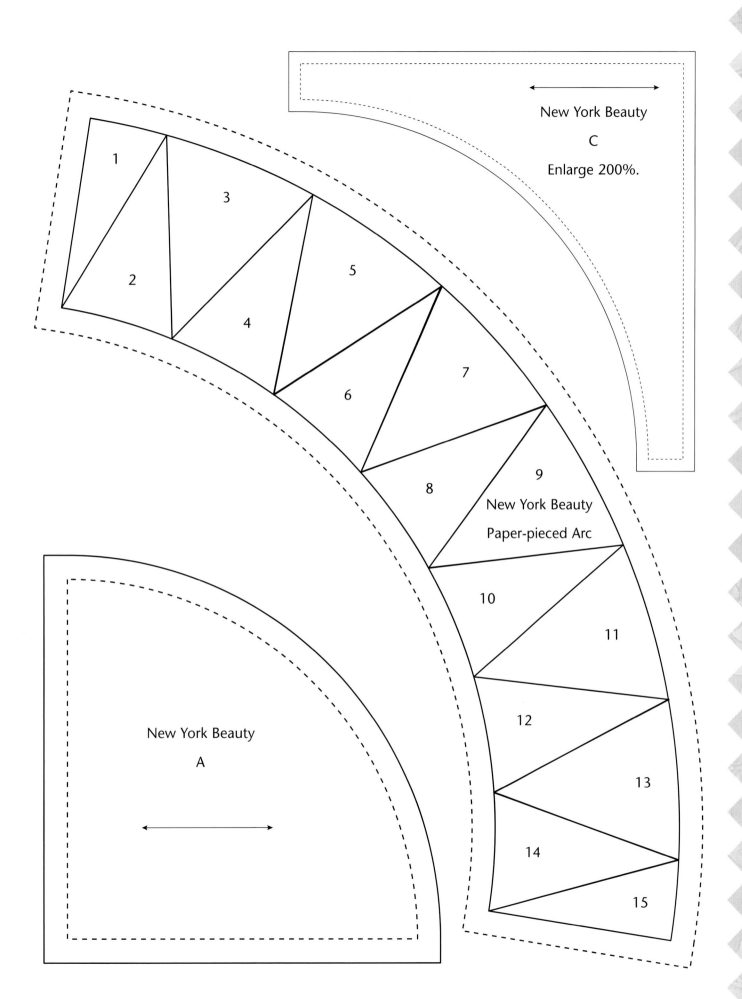

New York Beauty
C
Enlarge 200%.

1

3

2

5

4

6

7

8

9

New York Beauty
Paper-pieced Arc

10

11

12

13

14

15

New York Beauty
A

Finished Size: 36″ x 36″

Designed and machine quilted by Sue Vollbrecht, 2003.

WHOLECLOTH CRIB QUILT

From *The Quilter's Legacy*

FABRIC REQUIREMENTS

Solid white or cream: 2⅝ yards (includes backing and binding)

Batting: 40″ x 40″

CUTTING

Place the fabric on a flat surface, squaring-up 1 edge. Fold the lower corner up to the top edge and mark the place where the corner and edge meet. Cut fabric from selvage to selvage at this point, making a piece approximately 40″ square.

Set aside the rest of the fabric for backing and binding.

QUILT ASSEMBLY

1. Fold the fabric square in half horizontally and then in half vertically to find the center. Using that point as a reference, use a marking tool of your choice to lightly mark off a square 36″ x 36″ around the center. Lightly mark the horizontal and vertical divisions. Lightly mark the 2 diagonals.

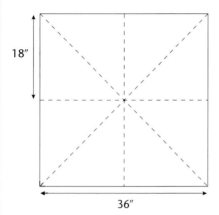

18″

36″

2. Enlarge the Center Plume pattern on page 56 by 200%. Following the placement guide on page 54, mark the central hearts and the feathered plume design in the center of the quilt.

3. Using the Feathered Heart pattern on page 55, mark the feathered heart design in each corner. The edges of the feathered hearts should be 2″ from the sides of the quilt.

4. Using the Elm Leaf Wreath pattern on page 56, mark the elm leaf wreath designs on each side of the quilt, 4″ from the edges.

5. Using the Ribbon pattern on page 55, mark the ribbon designs so they connect to the feathered hearts and elm leaf wreaths. Make 4 and 4 reversed.

6. Refer to Quilting 101, page 92, to layer the quilt top, batting, and backing. Baste. Quilt on the drawn lines either by hand or machine. Fill in the unmarked areas with stipple or meandering quilting or a design of your choice. Bind.

7. Sew a label to the back of your quilt providing your name and the **name** and birth date of the lucky **baby who** gets to snuggle in your **quilt. Be sure to atta**ch the tag secu**rely so that little** hands won't remove it!

*S*ummer would need better drawing skills than Sylvia possessed to create a picture that would do justice to Mother's third quilt, a white wholecloth quilt. A masterpiece of intricate quilting, it was so much smaller than the others that Sylvia might have assumed it was a crib quilt except that no infant had ever slept beneath it. Sylvia's memory and the quilt's pristine condition concurred on that point. If Mother had made it later in life, it could have been intended for a fourth child wished for but never conceived or even a grandchild, but Mother had completed it several years before Claudia had been born. Sylvia had always wondered why Mother had not given that beautiful quilt to her eldest child, and why she had not embroidered her initials and date on the back, the last, finishing touch she had added to all her other quilts.

Excerpted from *The Quilter's Legacy*
by Jennifer Chiaverini

Placement Guide

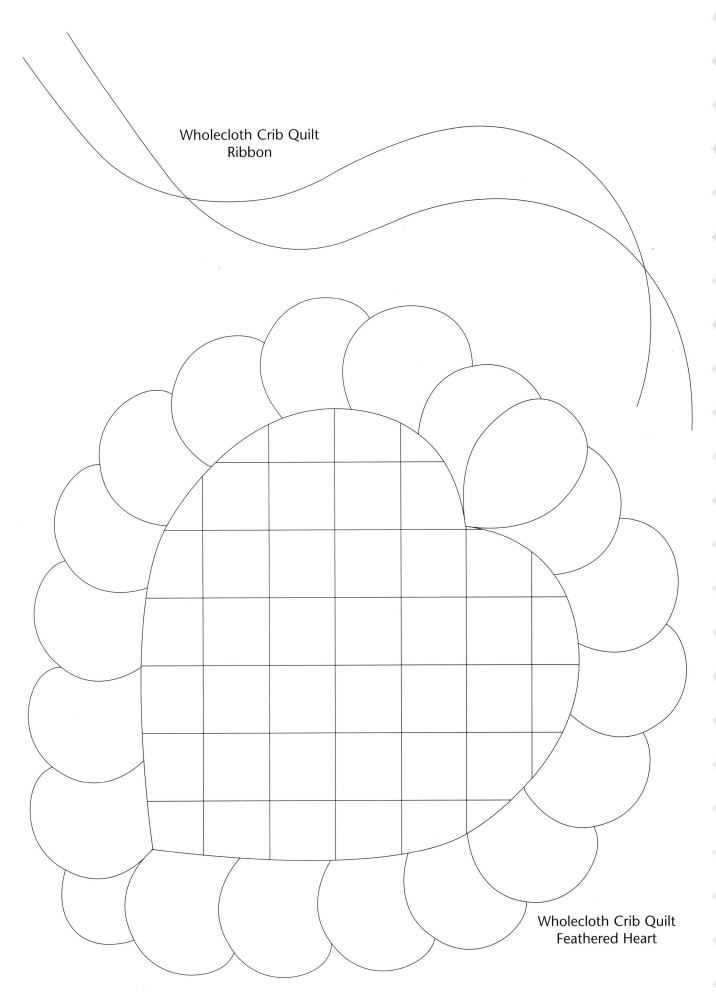

Wholecloth Crib Quilt
Ribbon

Wholecloth Crib Quilt
Feathered Heart

Wholecloth Crib Quilt
Center Plume

Enlarge 200%.

Wholecloth Crib Quilt
Elm Leaf Wreath

Finished Size: 56″ x 72″
Block Size: 16″ finished
Number of Blocks: 12

Machine pieced by Geraldine Neidenbach and Heather Neidenbach, machine quilted by Sue Vollbrecht, 2003.

Harriet Hargraves's "Vintage Indigoes" fabrics used in this quilt were generously donated by P&B Textiles.

ELEANOR'S OCEAN WAVES

From *The Quilter's Legacy*

FABRIC REQUIREMENTS

Assorted blue prints in hues varying from green-blue to blue-violet: 3½ yards (includes binding)

Assorted white and off-white background fabrics: 4¼ yards (includes border)

Batting: 60″ x 76″

Backing: 3⅛ yards

CUTTING

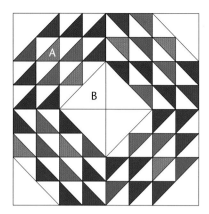

Ocean Waves block

Assorted blue prints: Cut 51 rectangles 6½″ x 9½″.

Cut 48 squares 2⅞″ x 2⅞″, then cut diagonally once to make 96 triangles.

White and off-white background fabrics: Cut 51 rectangles 6½″ x 9½″.

Cut 48 squares 2⅞″ x 2⅞″, then cut diagonally once to make 96 triangles. These are the small white triangles.

Cut 48 squares 4⅞″ x 4⅞″, then cut diagonally once to make 96 triangles. These are the large white triangles.

Cut 4 strips 2½″ wide. Sew strips together in pairs (see page 91), and cut a 2½″ x 64½″ border from each pair.

Cut 3 strips 2½″ wide. Sew diagonally end to end (see page 91), and cut 2 borders 2½″ x 52½″.

BLOCK ASSEMBLY

1. Pair 1 white rectangle with 1 blue rectangle, right sides together.

2. Using an accurate photocopier, make 51 copies of the triangle square quick-piecing grid on page 35. Securely pin a quick-piecing grid to the paired rectangles.

Note: If you prefer, you can reproduce the grid by hand by drawing it on the wrong side of each white rectangle before pairing it with a blue rectangle.

3. Stitching directly through the paper, sew on dashed line 1 in the directions of the arrows. Repeat for dashed line 2.

*A*long with the photograph of the baby, [Eleanor] had sent [Frederick] a picture of herself holding up her most recent quilt. She had chosen the Ocean Waves pattern for the ocean that separated them, blue and white fabrics for the crashing storm he faced abroad and the churning sea her life seemed without him. "Hurry home and help me use this, darling," she had written on the back, blushing as she imagined how his buddies would tease him.

Excerpted from *The Quilter's Legacy* by Jennifer Chiaverini

4. Separate the half-square triangle units by cutting on the solid lines. Remove the paper.

5. Press seams toward the blue fabric.

6. Repeat for the remaining white and blue rectangles to make 604 half-square triangle units.

7. Sew 2 rows of 2 half-square triangle units and 2 rows of 3 half-square triangle units. Sew 1 small blue triangle to a 2 square row and 1 to a 3 square row. Sew 1 small white triangle to a 2 square row and 1 to a 3 square row.

Note: Follow the diagram carefully to be sure the triangles are facing the correct direction.

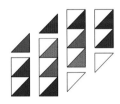

8. Sew the 4 rows together. Attach 2 large white triangles to opposite corners to make a quarter of the Ocean Waves block.

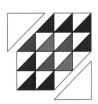

9. Repeat Steps 7 and 8 to make 3 more quarter blocks. Sew the 4 quarters together to complete the Ocean Waves block.

Note: Follow the diagram carefully to be sure the triangles are facing the correct direction.

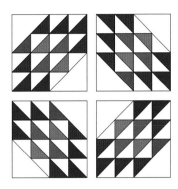

10. Repeat Steps 7–9 to make 12 Ocean Waves blocks.

QUILT ASSEMBLY

1. Sew the blocks into rows. Press the seams of alternate rows in opposite directions.

2. Sew the rows together. Press.

3. Refer to Quilting 101, page 91, for adding butted borders. Sew the white 2½″ x 64½″ borders to the sides of the quilt. Press the seams toward the borders.

4. Sew the white 2½″ x 52½″ borders to the top and bottom of the quilt. Press the seams toward the borders.

5. Sew half-square triangle units into 2 rows of 17 and 2 mirror-image rows of 17. Sew half-square triangle units into 2 rows of 14 and 2 mirror-image rows of 14. Press.

Make 2.

Make 2.

Make 2.

Make 2.

6. Sew the 2 longer mirror-image rows together to make a border of 34 half-square triangle units. Press. Repeat for second long border.

7. Sew the 2 shorter mirror-image rows together to make a border of 28 half-square triangle units. Press. Repeat for second short border.

8. Sew the longer borders to the sides of the quilt. Sew the shorter borders to the top and bottom of the quilt. Press the seams toward the inner border.

9. Refer to Quilting 101, page 92, to layer the quilt top, batting, and backing. Baste. Quilt as desired. Attach a hanging sleeve, if desired, and bind with blue binding.

10. Using permanent ink, make an identifying label for the back of your quilt.

Quilt Assembly Diagram

Finished Size: 82″ x 82″
Center Block Size: 38″ x 38″ finished

Hand appliquéd by June Pease,
quilted by Deb Randall, 2003.

ELMS AND LILACS

From *The Quilter's Legacy*

FABRIC REQUIREMENTS

Off-white (ecru): 8¾ yards for background and binding

Brown: ½ yard for vines and stems

Assorted medium to dark greens: 1 yard for elm leaves

Medium green: ½ yard for lilac leaves

Dark purple: ¾ yard to place under the lilac flowers for depth

Medium purple: 3 yards for lilac flowers and bias ribbons on borders

Pink: 1 yard for bias ribbons on borders

Batting: 86″ x 86″

Backing: 6 yards

CUTTING

Make templates from the patterns on pages 64–65.

Off-white (ecru): Cut 1 square 38½″ x 38½″ for the center block.

Cut 4 strips 6½″ x 55½″ for inner borders. Cut on the lengthwise grain of the fabric (parallel to the selvage edge). You will have no seams in your borders this way.

Cut 4 strips 16½″ x 87″ for the outer borders. Cut on the lengthwise grain of the fabric (parallel to the selvage edge).

From a 36″ x 36″ square, cut 2¼″-wide continuous bias binding for the scalloped edge of the quilt. Refer to Quilting 101, page 90.

Brown: Cut ¾″-wide continuous bias strips from a 16″ x 16″ square. Refer to Quilting 101, page 90, to make ¼″-wide bias for the stems and the vines.

Assorted medium to dark greens: Cut 14 elm leaves (A) for the center square and outer borders.

Cut 11 reverse sets of elm leaves (Ar) for the center square and outer borders.

Medium green: Cut 12 sets of lilac leaves (B) for outer borders.

Dark purple: Cut 7 sets of lilac blooms (B) for the center square and outer borders.

Cut 4 reverse sets of lilac blooms (Br) for outer borders.

Replace the center flower of lilac bloom (B) with large lilac (C), and cut 4 sets for the outer border.

Medium purple: Cut approximately 774 lilac flowers.

Cut 1″-wide continuous bias strips from a 28″ x 28″ square. Refer to Quilting 101, page 90, to make approximately 19½ yards (702″) of ⅜″-wide bias for the inner and outer borders.

Pink: Cut 1″-wide continuous bias strips from a 28″ x 28″ square. Refer to Quilting 101, page 90, to make approximately 19½ yards (702″) of ⅜″-wide bias for the inner and outer borders.

*M*onths ago, Fred and William had moved the quilt frame into the nursery so that [Eleanor] might quilt while she looked after the children. That was the excuse she made, but in truth, she did not want Fred to see the quilt she worked upon, a gift for their twentieth anniversary. Once she had not thought it possible she would live twenty years, and in a few weeks, she would have been married that long, more than half her life. It was a miracle, and she had Fred's love and God's grace to thank for it. She did not have the words to tell her Freddy what those twenty years had meant to her, so she stitched her love, her passion, her longing into the soft fabric, which was as yielding as they had learned to be with each other, and as strong, as closely woven together. She was the warp and he the weft of their married life, two souls who had chosen each other, not knowing the pattern their lives would form.

Excerpted from *The Quilter's Legacy*
by Jennifer Chiaverini

APPLIQUÉ

1. Refer to Quilting 101, page 90, for preparation for appliqué. Lightly mark the placement of the appliqué shapes on the center block, inner borders, and outer borders.

2. Use the patterns on pages 64–65 to prepare the appliqué pieces.

3. Beginning with the center block, appliqué stems and vines using the brown ¼″-wide bias strips. Next, appliqué the leaves.

Note: Leaves that are layered under other leaves are sewn down first. Appliqué the dark purple shapes under each lilac bloom. Now, appliqué medium purple lilac flowers over the dark purple shapes to complete each bloom.

4. Allowing room for the outer purple and pink appliquéd scalloped wave and the mitered corners, appliqué the stems and vines on a large outer border. Appliqué the leaves. Appliqué the dark purple under each of the lilac blooms. Appliqué the small flowers over the dark purple in each bloom. Repeat this border 3 more times.

5. Appliqué purple ⅜″-wide bias in a gentle curve down the center of an inner 6″-wide border strip. Appliqué the pink ⅜″-wide bias to the inner border, following the purple bias ribbon for placement. Repeat this border 3 more times.

QUILT ASSEMBLY

1. Refer to Quilting 101, page 91, for adding mitered borders. Sew the center block to the inner 6″-wide borders using ¼″ seam allowance. Miter the corners.

2. Sew the outer borders to the quilt using ¼″ seam allowance. Miter the corners of this border as well.

3. Appliqué the purple and pink bias ribbons to complete the design on the edge of the quilt. Using the scalloped wave of the appliquéd bias as a guide, mark a cutting line (remembering to add seam allowance) on the outer edge of this border (this is for placement of the binding).

4. Refer to Quilting 101, page 92, to layer the quilt top, batting, and backing. Baste. Quilt as desired.

5. Trim all layers of the quilt to the cutting line marked in Step 3. Attach a hanging sleeve, if desired, and bind.

6. Using permanent ink, make an identifying label for the back of your quilt.

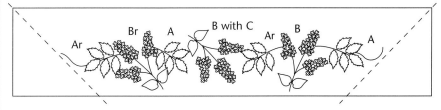

Outer Border Assembly Diagram

Center Block Assembly Diagram

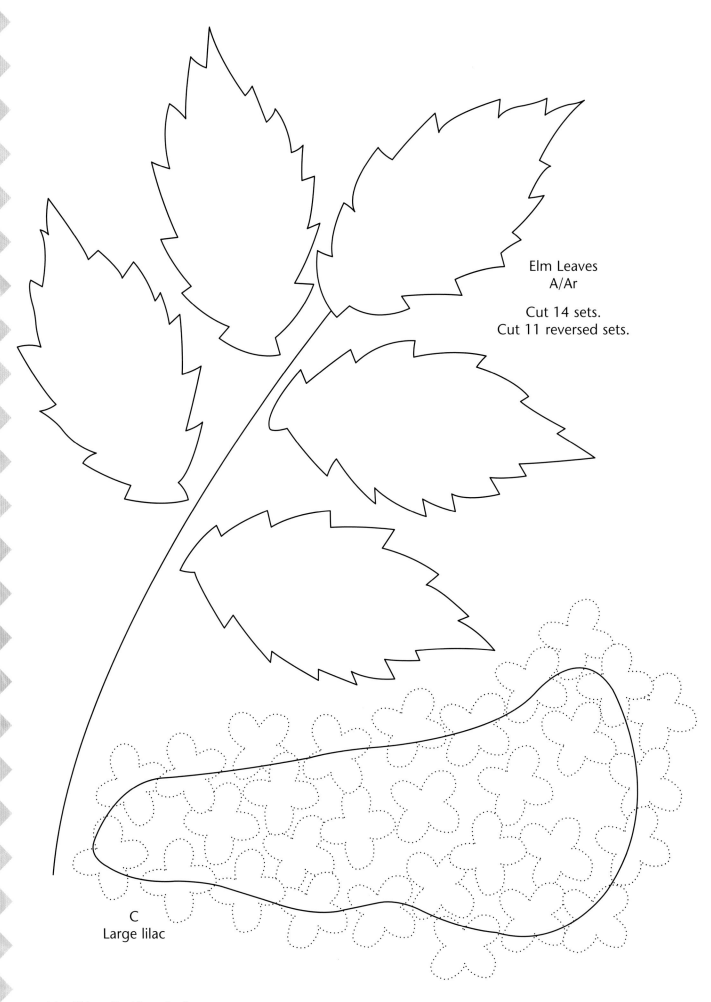

Elm Leaves
A/Ar

Cut 14 sets.
Cut 11 reversed sets.

C
Large lilac

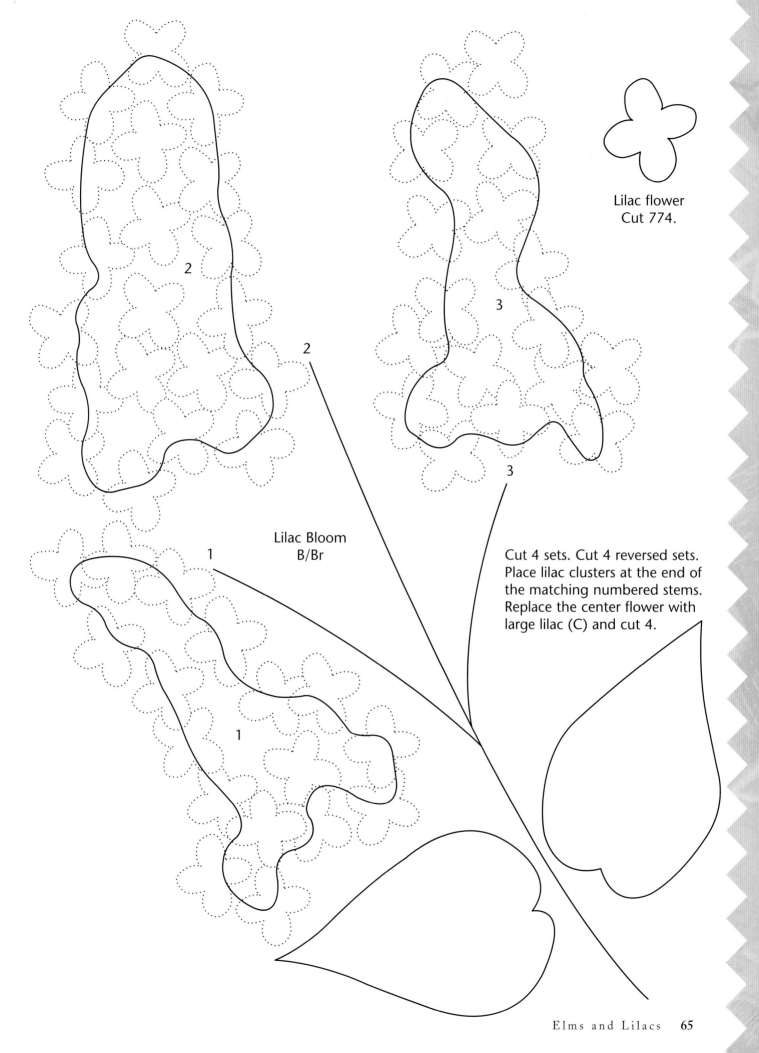

Lilac flower
Cut 774.

2

2

3

3

Lilac Bloom
B/Br

1

1

Cut 4 sets. Cut 4 reversed sets.
Place lilac clusters at the end of
the matching numbered stems.
Replace the center flower with
large lilac (C) and cut 4.

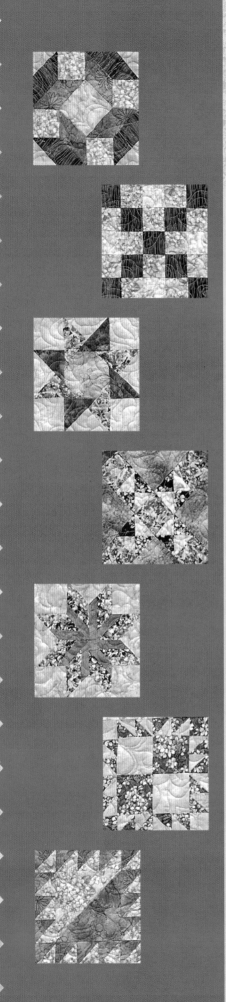

The MASTER QUILTER

In hindsight, it's remarkable that I ever felt this way, but when I wrote *The Master Quilter*, I thought it would be the last Elm Creek Quilts novel. In fact, that's why I chose the title. I had always planned to end the series with an allusion to a master quilter to complement the title of the first book, *The Quilter's Apprentice*. *The Master Quilter* completed a two-book contract with my publisher, and it seemed that it might be time to bring the adventures of the Elm Creek Quilters to an end. Therefore, I made sure to update readers on the happenings of all the Elm Creek Quilters and their families, as well as the Cross-Country Quilters and other favorite (and notorious) characters from the series.

With the publication of *The Quilter's Legacy*, however, my loyal readers assured me they were not at all ready to allow the series to conclude! *The Quilter's Legacy* received greater critical acclaim than any of my previous books, and for the first time, an Elm Creek Quilts novel reached the *New York Times* best-seller list. I was thrilled and gratified by this response, as any author would be, and decided to continue the series indefinitely. These characters are so real to me, and their lives so rich with detail and possibility, that I honestly believe I could write about them for many years to come.

In *The Master Quilter*, Sarah McClure and Summer Sullivan decide to make Sylvia and Andrew a bridal quilt by collecting 6″ sampler blocks from Sylvia's friends, colleagues, and admirers from around the world. Just as Sarah and Summer sought contributions for their quilt, I appealed to the Mad City Quilters, an Internet mailing list for Wisconsin quilters, and fans who met me on my book tour for help. Before I knew it, I had nearly eighty eager volunteers ready and willing to complete blocks for *Sylvia's Bridal Sampler*. Their piecing and appliqué skills were truly wonderful, and I was especially pleased to discover how much they enjoyed working with the fabric from my first fabric line from Red Rooster Fabrics, "Elm Creek Quilts—Sylvia's Collection." The roses and ivy, elm leaves, flowing water, and stone patterns evoke both Sylvia's personality and the natural beauty of Elm Creek Manor.

In all of my novels, even the ones with a contemporary setting, I can rarely resist indulging in a bit of quilt history, and *The Master Quilter* was no exception. In this story, Gwen Sullivan, Elm Creek Quilter and professor of American Studies at Waterford College, investigates the Sears Century of Progress Quilt Exhibition at the 1933 World's Fair held in Chicago. In my research, I found a wonderful book by Merikay Waldvogel and Barbara Brackman titled *Patchwork Souvenirs of the 1933 World's Fair*. Gwen's quilt block, Sylvia's Shooting Star, was inspired by a quilt featured in that book, although Mary Mihalovits Gasperik's quilt, *Star Arcturus*, apparently was not actually entered in the 1933 quilt competition.

As Gwen learns, Sylvia and her sister, Claudia, collaborated on an entry, a theme quilt they called *Chain of Progress* for the Odd Fellow's Chain border encircling a medallion of appliquéd pictorial blocks. Sylvia and Claudia's quilt inspired my design for the *Odd Fellow's Chain* quilt featured here, which was made by a talented Virginia quilter, Laura Blanchard.

Maxine Hameister: Chicago Pavements

Donna R. Johnsen: Bear's Paw, 54-40 or Fight

Sue Johnson: Rolling Star

Susie Klostermann: Odd Fellow's Chain, Rosebud

Elinor Koepcke: Bright Hopes

Carol Donis Krein: Northwind, Providence

Nancy Dunn Kurr: Grandmother's Pride

Becki Kurtz: Dutchman's Puzzle

Dianne L. Larson: Cut Glass Dish, Mother's Favorite, Puss in the Corner, Steps to the Altar

Linda Lazic: Grandmother's Fan, King David's Crown, Square and Star

Diane Liebenthal: Double Nine Patch, Snail's Trail

Nancy Linz: Lancaster Rose, New Mexico

Judith Litman: Album

Rita Loper: Ladies' Aid Album

Karen Mackowski: Wild Goose Chase

Nancy Martin: Corn and Beans

Mary B. Meier: Birds in the Air

Alli Mielcarek: Dogtooth Violet, Love in a Mist

Flo Mielcarek: Friendship Quilt, Hands All Around, Posies Round the Square, The Friendship Quilt

Janet C. Miller: Robbing Peter to Pay Paul, Silver and Gold

Sharon Miller: Autumn Leaf

Clare Nordman: Contrary Husband, True Lover's Knot

Suzanne Myers Otto: Contrary Wife, Yankee Puzzle

Isabel Pentony: Ohio Star

Terri Petasek: Cats and Mice, Glorified Nine Patch

Patty Pohlman: Follow the Leader

Carol M. Pruess: Sarah's Choice

Sharon Raimondo: Clay's Choice, Jack in the Box

Leslie Rector: Pinwheel

Betsey Rewey: Amethyst, Diamond Friendship, Irish Chain, Log Cabin, Mosaic No. 3, Pinwheel, Ribbon Star, Right Hand of Friendship, Wedding Ring

Rosemary Riederer: Children's Delight

Wendy Robertson: Oklahoma Dogwood

Marion Schey: Gentleman's Fancy

Gail Schlise: Mexican Star, Sickle

Rosemary Schmidt: Bride's Bouquet, Gulf Star

Nancy Schrader: Milky Way

Cindy Schramm: Odd Fellow's Patch

Pamela Schuster: Grandmother's Flower Garden, Kaleidoscope, Laurel Wreath, New York Beauty, Windblown Square

Pam Skaar: Aunt Sukey's Choice, Duck and Ducklings

Caraline Smith: Queen Charlotte's Crown

Suad Stratton: Nine-Patch

Joan Stuesser: Barrister's Block, Blazing Star, Chimneys and Cornerstones, Handy Andy, Lady of the Lake, Ocean Waves

Annette Tallard: Rambler, Sawtooth Star

Renee Hoffmann Thompson: Mrs. Cleveland's Choice

Sue Trepte: Broken Dishes, Friendship Star

Ann Tulip: Grape Basket

Carol A. Valenta: Arizona, Stamp Basket

Sue Vollbrecht: Kansas Troubles, Weathervane

Carol Walters: Hunter's Star, Tennessee

Judith H. Ward: Anvil, Rolling Stone

The 140 different blocks for this quilt were made by my friends and readers from across the United States. Many thanks to all who helped make this wonderful quilt possible! The following is a sampling of the blocks used in the final quilt. Please feel free to add your favorite blocks.

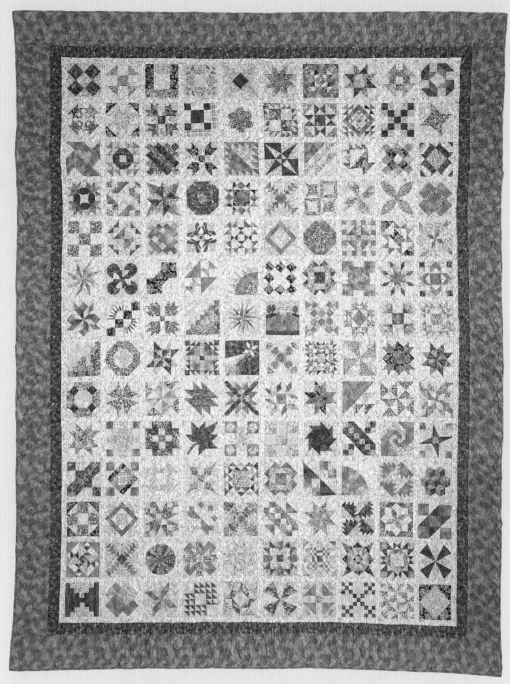

Finished Size: 87″ x 115″ or 115″ x 87″
Block Size: 6″ finished
Number of Blocks: 140

Machine pieced by Jennifer Chiaverini, machine quilted by Sue Vollbrecht, 2004.

The "Elm Creek Quilts—Sylvia's Collection" fabric used in this quilt were generously donated by Red Rooster Fabrics.

SYLVIA'S BRIDAL SAMPLER

From *The Master Quilter*

FABRIC REQUIREMENTS

Note: These figures are approximations only. The actual fabric quantities will depend on the blocks selected for the sampler.

Beiges: 10 yards (includes sashing and inner border)

Light roses: 1½ yards

Dark roses: 1½ yards

Light greens: 2 yards

Dark greens: 1½ yards (includes middle border)

Medium greens: 1½ yards

Light blues: 1½ yards

Medium blues: 4½ yards (includes outer border and binding)

Dark blues: 1½ yards

Medium tans: 1½ yards

Batting: 91″ x 119″

Backing: 7⅝ yards

GRACE'S FRIENDSHIP BLOCK

CUTTING

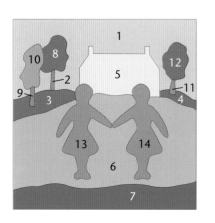

Light blue: Cut 1 square 8″ x 8″ for the block background (1).

Dark rose, dark blue, medium tan, dark green, and medium green: Use scraps at least ½″ larger on all sides than the corresponding appliqué shapes.

BLOCK ASSEMBLY

1. Refer to Quilting 101, page 90, for preparation for appliqué. Lightly mark the placement of the appliqué shapes on the background block (1).

2. Use the Grace's Friendship block pattern on page 76 to prepare the appliqué pieces. Cut the tree trunks (2, 9, 11) from medium tan, and cut the house (5) from beige. Cut 2 trees (8, 12) from dark green and 1 tree (10) from medium green. Cut the meadow (3, 4) from dark green. Cut the grass (6) from medium green. Cut the creek (7) from dark blue. Cut the women (13, 14) from dark rose.

3. Appliqué the shapes using your favorite method, following the numerical order on the pattern.

4. Trim the background block to 6½″ x 6½″ (includes seam allowance).

SARAH'S FAVORITE

CUTTING

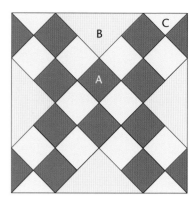

Make a template from pattern A on page 77.

Medium green: Cut 10 A's.

Cut 1 square 2¾″ x 2¾″, then cut diagonally twice to make 4 triangles (C).

Dark green: Cut 10 A's.

Cut 1 square 2¾″ x 2¾″, then cut diagonally twice to make 4 triangles (C).

Beige: Cut 1 square 4¼″ x 4¼″, then cut diagonally twice to make 4 triangles (B).

BLOCK ASSEMBLY

1. Sew 1 medium green square (A) to 1 dark green square (A). Press toward the dark fabric.

2. Sew the units together in pairs to make 5 Four-Patch blocks. Press.

Make 5.

3. Sew 3 Four-Patch blocks together to make a row. Press.

4. Sew 2 beige triangles (B) to opposite sides of 1 Four-Patch block. Press toward the triangles. Make 2 rows.

5. Sew the 3 rows together. Press.

6. Pair each light green triangle (C) with 1 dark green triangle to make C/C units. Make 2 C/C units, with the light green triangle on the left and the dark green on the right, and 2 mirror-image C/C units. Press toward the dark fabric.

7. Attach the 2 triangle units to the corners to complete the block. Press.

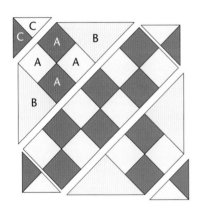

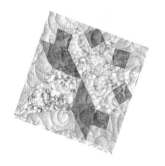

Bride's Bouquet Block

CUTTING

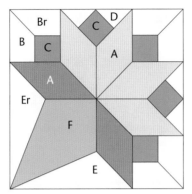

Make templates from the patterns on page 75.

Light rose: Cut 4 A's.

Dark rose: Cut 5 squares 1⅜″ x 1⅜″ (C).

Medium green: Cut 1 F.

Dark green: Cut 2 A's.

Beige: Cut 3 B's. Reverse the template and cut 3 Br's.

Cut 1 square 2½″ x 2½″, then cut diagonally twice to make 4 triangles (D).

Cut 1 E. Reverse the template and cut 1 Er.

BLOCK ASSEMBLY

1. Sew 2 beige triangles D to 1 dark rose square C. Make 2 D/C/D units.

2. Refer to Quilting 101, page 88, for Y-seam construction. Sew 2 light rose diamonds to 2 sides of a D/C/D unit. Take care to stitch from dot to dot without going into the seam allowance. Sew the 2 diamonds together. Make 2 A/D/C/D/A units.

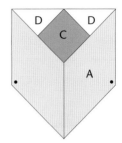

Make 2.

3. Stitching from dot to dot, sew 1 beige trapezoid (B) to a dark rose square (C). Using Y-seam construction, attach a Br trapezoid to the B/C unit. Make 3.

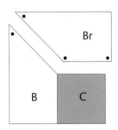

Make 3.

4. Sew the 2 A/D/C/D units together, stitching from point to point. Using Y-seam construction, attach a B/C/Br unit.

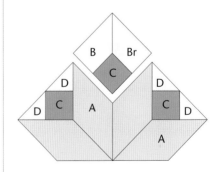

Bouquet Flowers Unit

5. Sewing from dot to dot, attach the other B/C/Br units to the unit created in Step 4.

6. Sewing from dot to dot, attach 1 dark green diamond (A) to the beige triangle E and 1 dark green diamond (A) to the beige triangle Er. Using Y-seam construction, attach both A/E units to the bouquet stem F.

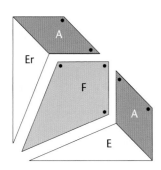

Bouquet Stem Unit

7. Using Y-seam construction, attach the Bouquet Stem unit to the Bouquet Flowers unit. Press the completed block.

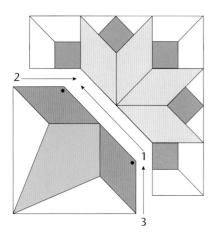

MOTHER'S DELIGHT BLOCK

CUTTING

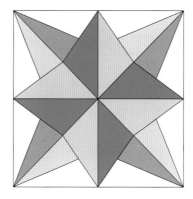

Cut light rose, dark rose, medium blue, dark blue, and beige pieces at least ¾″ larger on all sides than the corresponding paper-pieced shapes.

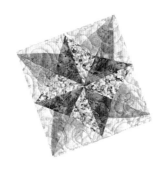

BLOCK ASSEMBLY

1. Refer to Quilting 101, page 89, for paper-piecing instructions. Make 4 copies of the Mother's Delight Foundation A and 4 copies of the Mother's Delight Foundation B on page 77.

2. Paper piece the 8 patterns, using the illustration as a guide for colors.

3. Sew together 1 Mother's Delight Foundation A and 1 Mother's Delight Foundation B to make a quarter block. Press seam open. Make 4 total.

4. Sew the 4 quarters together to complete the block. Press seams open. Remove the paper after the block is sewn into a quilt.

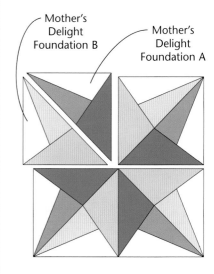

Mother's Delight Foundation B

Mother's Delight Foundation A

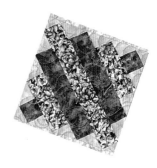

GRANDMOTHER'S PRIDE BLOCK

CUTTING

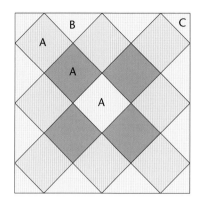

Make a template from pattern A on page 77.

Light rose: Cut 8 A's.

Dark rose: Cut 4 A's.

Beige: Cut 1 A.

Cut 2 squares 3¼" x 3¼", then cut diagonally twice to make 8 triangles (B).

Cut 2 squares 1⅞" x 1⅞", then cut diagonally once to make 4 triangles (C).

BLOCK ASSEMBLY

1. Sew the pieces into diagonal rows. Press seams toward the darker fabrics.

2. Sew the rows together. Press.

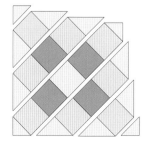

HANDY ANDY BLOCK

CUTTING

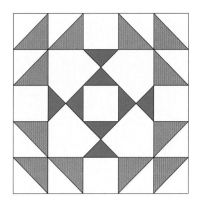

Cut medium tan, dark blue, and beige pieces at least ¾" larger on all sides than the corresponding paper-pieced shapes.

BLOCK ASSEMBLY

1. Refer to Quilting 101, page 89, for paper-piecing instructions. Make 2 copies each of the Handy Andy foundations A, C, and D and 1 copy of the Handy Andy foundation B on page 77.

2. Paper piece the 7 paper-piecing patterns, using the illustration as a guide for colors.

3. Sew together the 2 Handy Andy foundations A to B. Press seams open.

4. Attach the 2 Handy Andy foundations C to opposite sides of the Central Square unit created in Step 3. Press seams open.

*S*ylvia eagerly lifted the lid and dug through tissue paper until her hands touched fabric. "Oh, my word, I knew it. You ladies are wonderful."

Diane nudged Gwen. "She hasn't even seen it yet."

"She knows a quilt when she feels one," said Andrew, helping Sylvia unfold it.

Her friends came forward to take the edges of the quilt and hold it open between them. "Oh, my," said Sylvia, and then she could only clasp her hands to her heart in joy.

It was a sampler quilt top in blue, rose, lilac, and greens of every hue, all blending and contrasting harmoniously in a frame of LeMoyne Stars. Sylvia took in the arrangement of rows of blocks and quickly calculated that there were 140 blocks in every pieced and appliquéd pattern imaginable. Some of her favorites caught her eye: LeMoyne Star, Snow Crystals, Little Giant.

"It's very nice," said Andrew, "but you forgot to finish it." The women burst into laughter.

Excerpted from *The Master Quilter* by Jennifer Chiaverini

5. Sew the 2 Handy Andy foundations D to the top and bottom of the block. Press seams open.

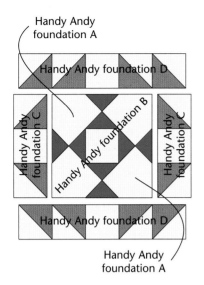

Handy Andy foundation A

Handy Andy foundation D

Handy Andy foundation C

Handy Andy foundation B

Handy Andy foundation C

Handy Andy foundation B

Handy Andy foundation D

Handy Andy foundation A

6. Remove the paper after the block is sewn into the quilt top.

SASHING AND BORDERS

CUTTING

Dark green: Cut 6 strips 2½″ wide. Sew diagonally end to end (see page 91), and cut 2 strips 2½″ x 99½″ for the middle long borders.

Cut 4 strips 2½″ wide. Sew strips together in pairs (see page 91), and cut a 2½ x 75½″ strip from each pair for the middle short borders.

Medium blue: Cut 7 strips 6½″ wide. Sew diagonally end to end, and cut 2 strips 6½″ x 103½″ for the outer long borders.

Cut 6 strips 6½″ wide. Sew diagonally end to end, and cut 2 strips 6½″ x 87½″ for the outer short borders.

Beige: Cut 5 strips 6½″ wide. Cut into 130 short sashing strips 1½″ x 6½″.

Cut 23 strips 1½″ wide. Sew diagonally end to end, and cut 9 long sashing strips 1½″ x 97½″.

Cut 5 strips 1½″ wide. Sew diagonally end to end, and cut 2 strips 1½″ x 97½″ for the inner long borders.

Cut 4 strips 1½″ wide. Sew strips together in pairs, and cut a 1½″ x 71½″ strip from each pair for the inner short borders.

QUILT ASSEMBLY

1. Make 134 additional 6″ (finished) sampler blocks.

Note: For best results, enlist the aid of friends!

2. Arrange the sampler blocks in 10 rows of 14 blocks. Sew blocks together with short sashing strips. Press seams toward the sashing strips.

Note: If any of the blocks have an obvious up-and-down orientation, decide whether you prefer a vertical or horizontal orientation for your quilt and arrange all directional blocks accordingly.

3. Sew the sampler block rows together, separated by the long sashing strips. Press toward the sashing strips.

4. Refer to Quilting 101, page 91, for adding butted borders. Sew the long dark beige inner borders to the long sides of the quilt. Sew the short dark beige inner borders to the short sides of the quilt. Press toward the border.

5. Sew the long dark green middle borders to the long sides of the quilt. Sew the short dark green middle borders to the long sides of the quilt. Press toward the green border.

6. Sew the long medium blue outer borders to the long sides of the quilt. Sew the short medium blue outer borders to the long sides of the quilt. Press seams toward blue border.

7. Refer to Quilting 101, page 92, to layer the quilt top, batting, and backing. Baste. Quilt as desired. Attach a hanging sleeve, and bind.

Note: If you are using signature squares, these can be pieced together to make the quilt backing.

8. If you did not use signature squares for the quilt backing, make a panel including the names of all the block contributors. Appliqué to the back of the quilt.

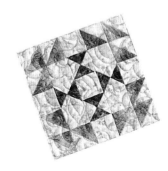

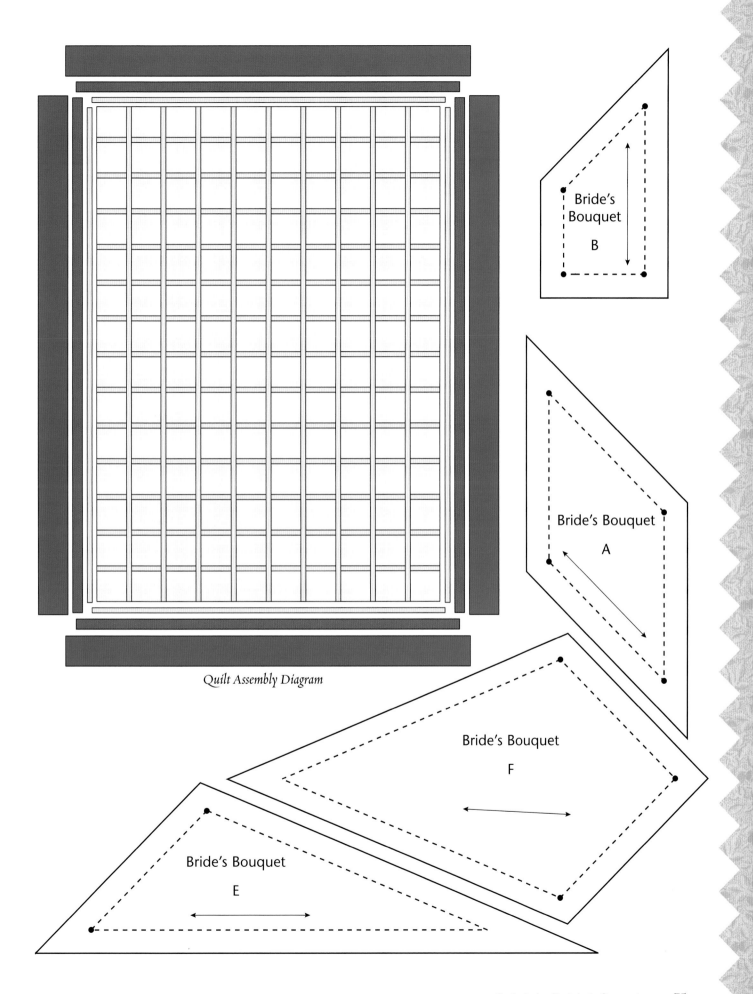

Quilt Assembly Diagram

Bride's Bouquet

B

Bride's Bouquet

A

Bride's Bouquet

F

Bride's Bouquet

E

Grace's Friendship Block

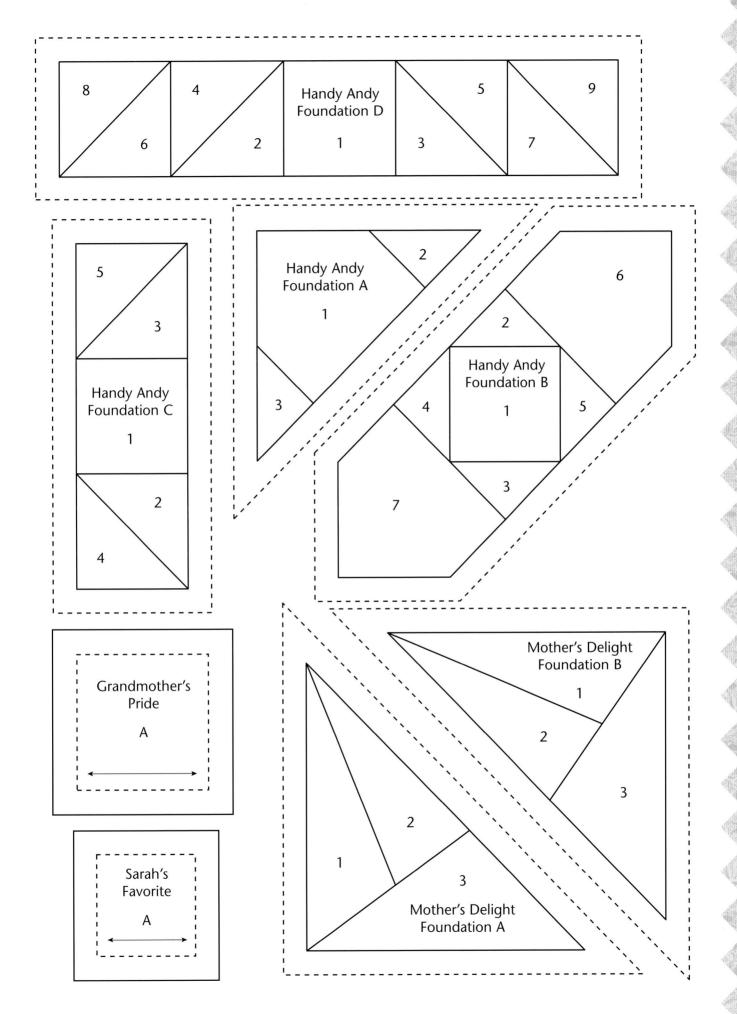

Finished Size: 74″ x 98″
Block Sizes: 12″ Shooting Star finished, 6″ LeMoyne Star finished
Number of Blocks: 17 Shooting Star, 21 LeMoyne Star

Machine pieced by Jennifer Chiaverini,
machine quilted by Sue Vollbrecht, 2003.

SYLVIA'S SHOOTING STAR

From *The Master Quilter*

FABRIC REQUIREMENTS

Blue tone-on-tone: 7 yards (includes outer border and binding)

Dark gold: 1¼ yards

Medium gold: 1½ yards

Light gold: 2⅛ yards (includes inner border)

Yellow: 1 yard

Batting: 78″ x 102″

Backing: 6½ yards

CUTTING

Make templates from patterns on page 82.

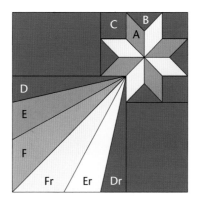

Shooting Star block

Blue tone-on-tone: Cut 18 squares 12½″ x 12½″.

Cut 6 strips 4¾″ wide, then cut into 34 rectangles 4¾″ x 6½″.

Cut 4 strips 2¼″ wide, then cut into 67 squares 2¼″ x 2¼″ (C).

Cut 2 strips 3¾″ wide, cut into 21 squares 3¾″ x 3¾″, then cut diagonally twice to make 84 triangles (B).

Cut 17 D's. Reverse the template and cut 17 Dr's.

Cut 5 strips 6½″ wide. Sew diagonally end to end (see page 91), and cut 2 borders 6½″ x 86½″.

Cut 4 strips 6½″ wide. Sew strips together in pairs (see page 91), and cut a 6½″ x 62½″ border from each pair.

Dark gold: Cut 17 E's.

Cut 6 strips 1¾″ wide, layer the strips, and trim one end at a 45° angle. Cut 84 diamonds (A).

Medium gold: Cut 17 F's.

Light gold: Reverse template F and cut 17 Fr's.

Cut 5 strips 1½″ wide. Sew diagonally end to end (see page 91), and cut 2 borders 1½″ x 84½″.

Cut 4 strips 1½″ wide. Sew strips together in pairs (see page 91), and cut a 1½″ x 62½″ border from each pair.

Cut 6 strips 1¾″ wide, layer the strips, and trim one end at a 45° angle. Cut 84 diamonds (A).

Yellow: Reverse template E and cut 17 Er's.

*S*ylvia insisted that each of her friends point out her block and explain why she chose it. …

"This one is mine." Gwen indicated a block near the center of the quilt. Sylvia did not recognize the pattern, which resembled a gold comet streaking across a sunset-violet sky. "I adapted it from a design in a quilt entered in the 1933 World's Fair quilt competition. I chose it because while Sylvia is definitely an original, her art and influences are deeply rooted in quilting's oldest and best traditions. Since I don't know the original name of the block, I call it Sylvia's Shooting Star."

Excerpted from *The Master Quilter*
by Jennifer Chiaverini

BLOCK ASSEMBLY

1. Refer to Quilting 101, page 88, for Y-seam construction. Sew a light gold diamond (A) and a dark gold diamond (A) to opposite sides of a blue triangle (B). Take care not to sew into the seam allowance. Make 84 A/B/A units.

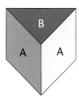

Make 84.

2. Sew 1 blue square (C) to the light gold diamond of the A/B/A unit, taking care not to sew into the seam allowance. Make 67 A/B/A/C units. Set aside the 17 remaining A/B/A units.

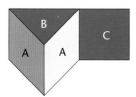

Make 67.

3. Sew together 2 A/B/A/C units to make a block half, stitching from the outer edge to the dot, in the direction of the arrows. Press. Make 25 block halves.

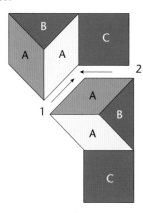

Make 25.

4. Sew together 2 block halves. Press. Repeat to make 4 complete LeMoyne Star blocks. Set aside for the outer border.

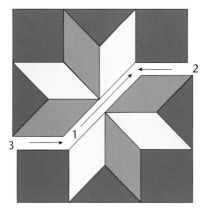

Make 4.

5. Sew together the 17 remaining A/B/A/C units and the 17 remaining A/B/A units.

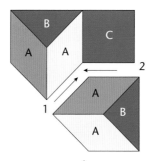

Make 17.

6. Sew together the 17 units created in Step 5 with the 17 block halves created in Step 3.

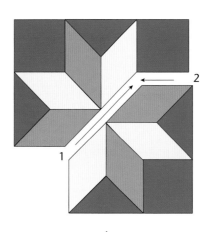

Make 17.

7. Attach 2 rectangles 4¾″ x 6½″ to each of the units created in Step 6.

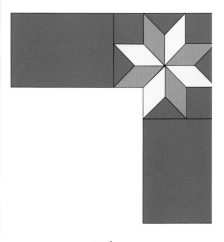

Make 17.

8. Sew together triangles D, E, and F. Sew together triangles Fr, Er, and Dr. Sew the 2 units together to make a Star Trail unit. Make 17.

9. Using Y-seam construction, sew 1 Star Trail unit to each of the partial blocks created in Step 7. Press. Make 17.

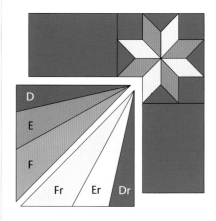

Make 17.

QUILT ASSEMBLY

1. Sew the blocks into rows, alternating with blue setting squares. Press the seams toward the blue squares.

2. Sew the rows together. Press.

3. Refer to Quilting 101, page 91, for adding butted borders. Sew the light gold 1½″ x 84½″ borders to the sides of the quilt. Press the seams toward the borders.

4. Sew the 1½″ x 62½″ light gold borders to the top and bottom of the quilt. Press the seams toward the borders.

5. Sew the 6½″ x 86½″ blue borders to the sides of the quilt. Press the seams toward the blue borders.

6. Sew 2 LeMoyne Stars to the ends of each 6½″ x 62½″ blue border strip. Press toward the border. Sew the borders to the top and bottom of the quilt. Press the seams toward the borders.

7. Refer to Quilting 101, page 92, to layer the quilt top, batting, and backing. Baste. Quilt as desired. Attach a hanging sleeve, and bind with blue binding.

8. Sign and date your quilt on the back in permanent ink.

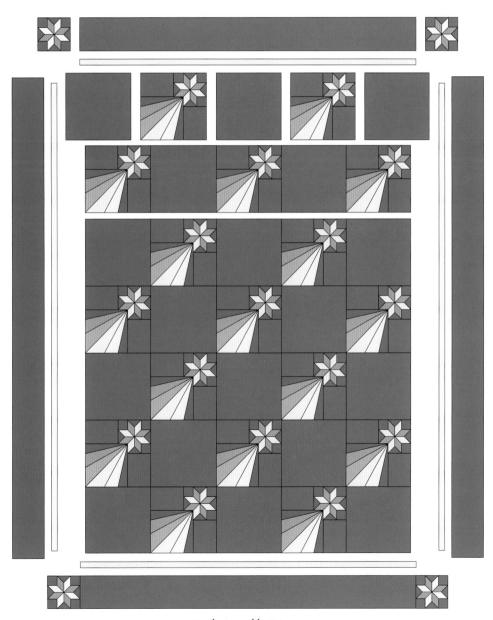

Quilt Assembly Diagram

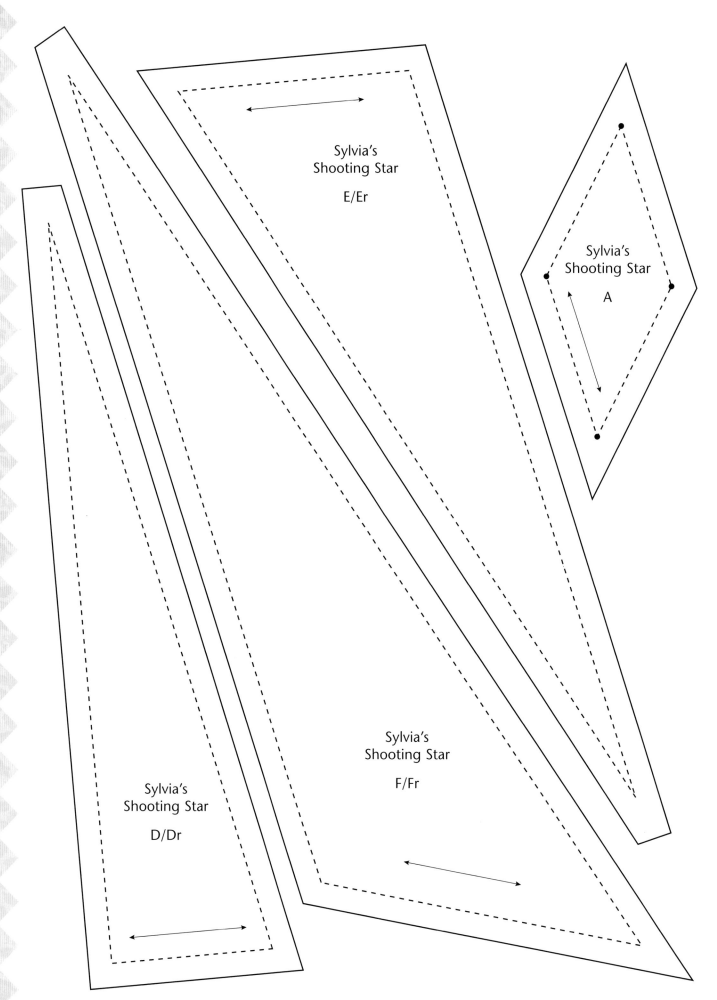

Sylvia's
Shooting Star

E/Er

Sylvia's
Shooting Star

A

Sylvia's
Shooting Star

F/Fr

Sylvia's
Shooting Star

D/Dr

Finished Size: 75″ x 91″

Block Size: 16″ finished

Number of Blocks: 20

Machine pieced and quilted by Laura Blanchard, 2003.

ODD FELLOW'S CHAIN

From *The Master Quilter*

FABRIC REQUIREMENTS

Backgrounds (cream, light beige, and light tan): 20 assorted fat quarters

Purple: 10 assorted fat quarters

Green: 10 assorted fat quarters

Red: 10 assorted fat quarters, plus 2½ yards for borders and binding

Gold: 10 assorted fat eighths

Batting: 79″ x 95″

Backing: 5⅓ yards

CUTTING

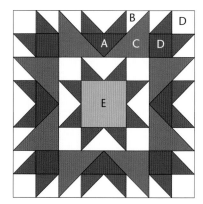

Odd Fellow's Chain block

Backgrounds: Cut 2 strips 2½″ x 21″ from each fat quarter, then cut into 160 rectangles 2½″ x 4½″ for the Flying Geese units.

Cut 1 strip 2⅞″ x 21″ from each of 12 background fat quarters, then cut into 80 squares 2⅞″ x 2⅞″. Cut diagonally once to yield 160 half-square triangles (B).

Cut 1 strip 2⅞″ x 21″ from each of 12 background fat quarters, then cut into 80 squares 2⅞″ x 2⅞″ for half-square triangle construction.

Cut 1 strip 2½″ x 21″ from each of 14 background fat quarters, then cut into 112 squares 2½″ x 2½″ (D).

Purple: Cut 4 strips 2½″ x 21″ from each of 10 purple fat quarters, then cut into 320 squares 2½″ x 2½″ for the Flying Geese units.

Cut a total of 12 strips 2⅞″ x 21″ from the 10 purple fat quarters, then cut the strips into 80 squares 2⅞″ x 2⅞″ for half-square triangle construction.

Green: Cut 2 strips 4⅞″ x 21″ from each of the green fat quarters, then cut strips into 80 squares 4⅞″ x 4⅞″. Cut diagonally once to make 160 half-square triangles (C).

The design itself was a compromise, Sylvia explained. Sylvia had wanted to create an original pictorial quilt inspired by the "Century of Progress" theme, but Claudia thought they would stand a better chance of pleasing the judges if they used a traditional pattern and devoted their time to flawless, intricate needlework rather than novelty. After an argument spanning several weeks which would have been better spent sewing, they agreed that Sylvia could design a central appliqué medallion depicting various scenes from colonial times until the present day, to which Claudia would add a border of pieced blocks. "Odd Fellow's Chain," said Sylvia, fingering the border. "Obviously, she chose it for its appearance, not its name."

"Unless she meant to make a statement about contemporary notions of progress."

"Hmph." Sylvia showed a hint of a smile. "Claudia was not that clever. The block did give us the quilt's title, however. We called it 'Chain of Progress.'"

Gwen draped the quilt over an upholstered armchair to better examine it. She could see in this early example of Sylvia's work how her tastes and skills had developed through the decades. The uneven quality of the needlework Gwen attributed to the widely differing abilities of the two sisters, but even the worst pieced Odd Fellow's Chain block proved that Claudia could not have been as poor a quilter as Sylvia suggested. The green Ribbon of Merit still attached to the quilt attested to that.

Excerpted from *The Master Quilter*
by Jennifer Chiaverini

Red: Cut 1 strip 2½″ x 21″ from each fat quarter. Cut strips into 80 squares 2½″ x 2½″ (D).

Cut 2 squares 5¼″ x 5¼″ from each fat quarter. Cut squares diagonally twice to yield 80 quarter-square triangles (A).

Cut 5 strips 6″ wide. Sew diagonally end to end (see page 91), and cut 2 borders 6″ x 80½″.

Cut 5 strips 6″ wide. Sew diagonally end to end and cut 2 borders 6″ x 75½″.

Gold: Cut 1 strip 2½″ x 21″ from each fat eighth, then cut into 48 squares 2½″ x 2½″ (D).

Cut 1 strip 4½″ x 21″ from each fat eighth, then cut into 20 squares 4½″ x 4½″ (E).

BLOCK ASSEMBLY

1. Refer to Quilting 101, page 88, for making the Flying Geese units. Use the 2½″ x 4½″ background rectangles and the 2½″ purple squares. Make 160 Flying Geese units. Set aside 80 for the Star units.

2. Sew a background triangle (B) to each side of the 80 remaining Flying Geese units. Press toward the B triangles.

Make 80.

3. Sew a red triangle (A) to the bottom of the Flying Geese unit as shown. Press toward the red triangle.

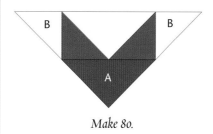

Make 80.

4. Sew a green triangle (C) to each side to complete the unit. Press toward the green triangles. Make 4 A/B/C units for each block (80 total).

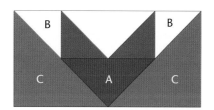

Make 80.

5. Draw a diagonal line on the wrong side of each 2⅞″ background square. Pair each 2⅞″ background square with a 2⅞″ purple square. Place squares right sides facing. Stitch ¼″ from each side of the drawn line. Cut on the drawn line. Press toward the purple triangle. Make 160 half-square triangle units.

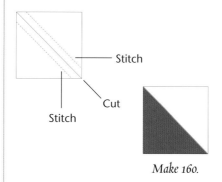

Make 160.

6. Sew a 2½″ background square (D), a 2½″ red square (D), and 2 half-square triangle units, as shown. Press. Make 32.

7. Sew a 2½″ gold square (D), a 2½″ red square (D), and 2 half-square triangle units, as shown. Press. Make 48.

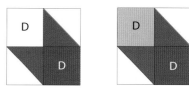

Make 32.   *Make 48.*
Block Corner Units

8. Make the Star units using 4 background 2½″ squares (D), 4 Flying Geese units (reserved from Step 1), and 1 gold 4½″ square (E). Sew units together, as shown. Press. Make 20.

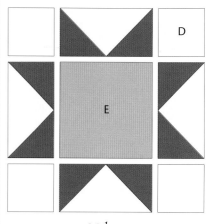

Make 20.
Star Unit

9. Following the block assembly diagrams, arrange 4 A/B/C units from Step 4, 4 Block Corner units, and 1 Star unit for each block. Sew units together to complete 20 blocks. Press.

Note: Block I contains 1 Gold Block Corner unit, Block II contains 2 Gold Block Corner units, and Block III contains 4 Gold Block Corner units.

Block I, Make 4.

Block II, Make 10.

Block III, Make 6.

QUILT ASSEMBLY

1. Arrange Blocks I, II, and III as shown in the quilt assembly diagram. Sew the blocks into rows. Press the seams of alternate rows in opposite directions.

2. Sew the rows together. Press.

3. Refer to Quilting 101, page 91, for adding butted borders. Sew the red 6″ x 80½″ borders to the long sides of the quilt. Press toward the border.

4. Sew the red 6″ x 75½″ borders to the top and bottom of the quilt. Press toward the border.

5. Refer to Quilting 101, page 92, to layer the quilt top, batting, and backing. Baste. Quilt as desired. Attach a hanging sleeve, and bind with red binding.

6. Using permanent ink, make an identifying label for the back of your quilt.

Quilt Assembly Diagram

QUILTING
101

Fabric requirements are based on a 42" width. Many fabrics shrink when washed, and widths vary by manufacturer. In cutting instructions, strips are usually cut on the crosswise grain, unless otherwise noted.

Seam Allowances: A ¼" seam allowance is used throughout. It's a good idea to do a test seam before you begin sewing to check that your ¼" is accurate.

Pressing: In general, press seams toward the darker fabric. Press lightly in an up-and-down motion. Avoid using a very hot iron or over-ironing, which can distort shapes and blocks.

Flying Geese: Mark a diagonal line on each square. With right sides facing, sew a square to one side of the rectangle on the marked diagonal line. Trim the excess to a ¼" seam allowance. Fold the square back, and press along the diagonal seam. Sew a square to the opposite side of the rectangle on the marked diagonal line. Trim the excess fabric to a ¼" seam allowance. Fold back, and press along the diagonal seam.

Sew and trim.

Press.

Sew and trim.

Y-Seam Construction: Mark a dot on the wrong side of the fabric ¼" from the point of the triangle, and then mark a dot ¼" from the corner of each diamond. This is the starting and stopping point of the Y-seam. Sew a diamond to the triangle unit. Backstitch at the dot. Press toward the diamond. Sew the other diamond to the opposite side of the triangle. Sew the two diamonds together, backstitching at the dot. Press.

Mark dots on the triangle and on the diamonds.

Stitch to the dot and backstitch.

Press toward the diamond.

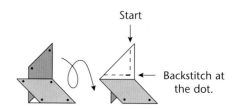

Flip over and sew the other diamond to the triangle.

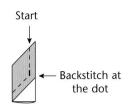

Sew the 2 diamonds together.

Press.

Paper Piecing: Once you get used to it, paper piecing is an easy way to ensure that your blocks will be accurate. You sew on the side of the paper with the printed lines. Fabric is placed on the nonprinted side. With paper piecing, you don't have to worry about the fabric grain. You are stitching on paper, which stabilizes the block. The paper is not removed until after the quilt top is together.

1. Trace or photocopy the number of paper-piecing patterns needed for your project.

2. Use a smaller-than-usual stitch length (1.5–1.8, or 18–20 stitches per inch) and a slightly larger needle (size 90/14). This makes the paper removal easier and will result in tighter stitches that cannot be pulled apart when you tear off the paper.

3. Cut the pieces slightly larger than necessary—about ¾″ larger or more for triangles. They do not need to be perfect shapes—one of the joys of paper piecing!

4. Follow the number sequence when piecing. Pin piece 1 in place on the blank side of the paper, but make sure you don't place the pin anywhere near a seamline. Hold the paper up to the light to make sure that the piece covers the area it is supposed to and that the seam allowance is amply covered.

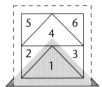

5. Fold the pattern back at the stitching line, and use a small acrylic ruler and a rotary cutter to trim the fabric to a ¼″ seam allowance.

6. Cut piece 2 large enough to cover the area of 2 plus a generous seam allowance. It helps to cut each piece larger than you think necessary; it might be a bit wasteful, but it's easier than ripping out tiny stitches! Align the edge with the trimmed seam allowance of piece 1, right sides facing, and pin. With the paper side up, stitch on the line between piece 1 and 2.

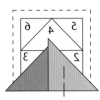

7. Open piece 2 and press.

8. Continue stitching each piece in order, being sure to fold back the paper pattern and trim the seam allowance to ¼″ before adding the next piece.

9. Trim all around the finished unit to the ¼″ seam allowance. Leave the paper intact until after the blocks have been sewn together, then carefully remove it. Creasing the paper at the seamline helps when tearing it.

Paper-Piecing Hints

- When making several identical blocks, it helps to work in assembly-line fashion. Add pieces 1 and 2 to each of the blocks, then add 3, and so on.

- Precutting all the pieces at once is a time-saver. Make one block first to ensure that each fabric piece will cover the area needed.

- To trim the seam, use a card or an envelope placed along the stitching line when folding the pattern back.

- Sometimes the seam allowance needs to be pressed toward the light fabric when dark and light pieces are sewn together, and the edge of the dark seam allowance might show through the light fabric. To prevent this, trim the dark seam allowance about ¹⁄₁₆″ narrower than the light seam allowance.

Preparation for Appliqué: To prepare the background for appliqué, lightly press the background block in half diagonally, vertically, and horizontally to find the center of the block and to create placement guidelines.

Using the patterns provided, trace each appliqué shape onto the template plastic or freezer paper and cut out on the line. Place the appliqué templates onto the background and lightly mark the background ⅛″ inside the sewing line.

Trace around the templates onto the desired appliqué fabric, adding a scant ¼″ seam allowance. Cut out the pieces along the pencil line.

Bias Stems and Vines: With wrong sides together, fold the bias strips in half lengthwise, and sew about ⅛″ from the outside edge. Insert a bias bar, and press on both sides, with the seam centered on the back. Remove the bias bar. Appliqué the bias strip in place with the seam down.

Continuous Bias Strips: The advantage to this method is that when the bias strip is cut, it is one continuous seamed strip. This is useful for bias stems, vines, and binding. Cut the fabric for the bias so it is a square. If yardage is ½ yard, cut an 18″ x 18″ square. Cut the square in half diagonally, creating two triangles.

Sew these triangles together as shown, using a ¼″ seam allowance. Press the seam open.

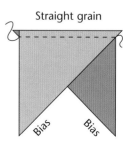

Straight grain

Bias   Bias

Using a ruler, mark the parallelogram, with lines spaced the width you need to cut your bias. Cut about 5″ along the first line.

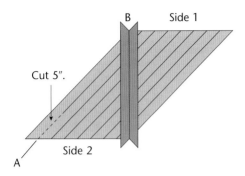

Join Side 1 and Side 2 to form a tube. Line A will line up with the raw edge at B, allowing the first line to be offset by 1 strip width. Pin the raw ends together, making sure that the lines match. Sew with a ¼″ seam allowance. Press seams open. Cut along drawn lines, creating one continuous strip.

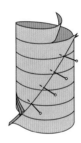

Diagonal Pieced Seams: When strips are to be cut on the crosswise grain, diagonally piece the strips together to achieve the needed lengths.

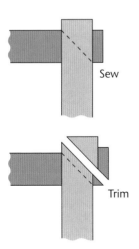

Butted Borders: In most cases, the side borders are sewn on first. When you have finished the quilt top, measure it vertically through the center. This will be the length for the side borders. Place pins at the centers of all four sides of the quilt top, as well as in the center of each side border strip. Pin the side borders to the quilt top first, matching the center pins. Using a ¼″ seam allowance, sew the borders to the quilt top and press.

Measure horizontally across the center of the quilt top, including the side borders. This will be the length for the top and bottom borders. Repeat pinning, sewing, and pressing.

Mitered Borders: Measure the length of the quilt top and add two times the width of your border, plus 5″. This is the length for the side borders.

Place pins at the centers of both side borders and at all four sides of the quilt top. From the center pin, measure in both directions and mark half of the measured length of the quilt top on both side borders. Pin by matching centers and the marked length of the side border to the edges of the quilt top. Stitch the strips to the sides of the quilt top. Stop and backstitch at the seam allowance line ¼″ in from the edge. The excess length will extend beyond each edge. Press seams toward the border.

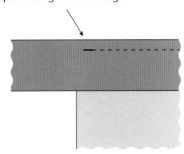

Determine the length needed for the top and bottom border the same way, measuring the width of the quilt top through the center, including both side borders. Add 5″ to this measurement. Cut or piece these border strips.

From the center of each border strip, measure in both directions and mark half of the measured width of the quilt top. Again, pin, stitch up to the ¼″ seamline, and backstitch. The border strips extend beyond each end.

To create the miter, lay the corner on the ironing board. Working with the quilt right side up, lay 1 strip on top of the adjacent border.

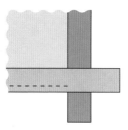

Fold the top border strip under itself so that it meets the edge of the outer border and forms a 45° angle. Press and pin the fold in place.

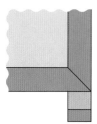

Fold under at a 45° angle.

Position a 90° angle triangle or ruler over the corner to check that the corner is flat and square. When everything is in place, press the fold firmly.

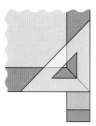

Square the corner.

Fold the center section of the top diagonally from the corner, right sides together, and align the long edges of the borders. On the wrong side, place pins near the pressed fold in the corner to secure the border strips.

Beginning at the inside corner, backstitch, then stitch along the fold toward the outside point, being careful not to allow any stretching to occur. Backstitch at the end. Trim the excess border fabric to ¼″ seam allowance. Press the seam open.

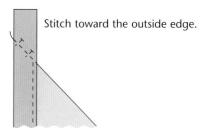

Stitch toward the outside edge.

Wrong side of quilt

Backing: Plan to make the backing a minimum of 2″ larger than the quilt top on all sides. Prewash the fabric, and trim the selvages before you sew the backing sections together. To economize, you can sew the back from any leftover fabrics or blocks in your collection.

Batting: The type of batting to use is a personal decision; consult your local quilt shop. Cut batting approximately 2″ larger on all sides than your quilt top.

Layering: Spread the backing wrong side up and tape the edges down with masking tape. (If you are working on carpet, you can use T-pins to secure the backing to the carpet.) Center the batting on top, smoothing out any folds. Place the quilt top right side up on top of the batting and backing, making sure it's centered.

If you plan to machine quilt, pin baste the quilt layers together with safety pins placed a minimum of 3″ to 4″ apart. Begin basting in the center, and move toward the edges first in vertical, then horizontal, rows.

If you plan to hand quilt, baste the layers together with thread using a long needle and light-colored thread. Knot one end of the thread. Using stitches approximately the length of the needle, begin in the center, and move out toward the edges.

Quilting: Whether by hand or machine, quilting enhances the pieced or appliqué design of the quilt. You may choose to quilt in-the-ditch, echo the pieced or appliquéd motifs, use patterns from quilting design books and stencils, or do your own free-motion quilting.

Double-Fold Straight Grain Binding (French Fold):

Trim excess batting and backing from the quilt. If you want a ¼″ finished binding, cut the strips 2¼″ wide and sew together with a diagonal seam to make a continuous binding strip.

Press the seams open, then press the entire strip in half lengthwise with wrong sides facing. With raw edges even, pin the binding to the edge of the quilt a few inches from the corner, and leave the first few inches of the binding unattached. Start sewing, using a ¼″ seam allowance.

Stop ¼″ from the first corner, and backstitch one stitch. Lift the presser foot and rotate the quilt. Fold the binding at a right angle so it extends straight above the quilt. Then bring the binding strip down even with the edge of the quilt. Begin sewing at the folded edge.

Stitch to ¼″ from corner.

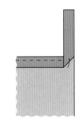

First fold for miter.

Second fold alignment.
Repeat in the same manner at all corners.

When you reach the beginning, fold the ending tail of the binding back on itself where it meets the beginning binding tail. From the fold, measure and mark the cut width of your binding strip. Cut the ending binding tail to this measurement. For example, if your binding is cut 2¼″ wide, measure from the fold on the ending tail of the binding 2¼″ and cut the binding tail to this length.

Open both tails. Place one tail on top of the other tail at right angles, right sides facing. Mark a diagonal line and stitch on the line. Trim the seam to ¼″. Press open.

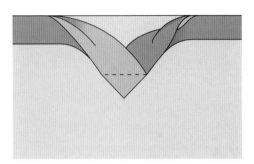

Stitch ends of binding diagonally.

Continue stitching the binding to the quilt. Fold the binding over the raw edges to the quilt back, and hand stitch, mitering the corners.

INDEX

Resources

Cory, Pepper. *Mastering Quilt Marking: Marking Tools & Techniques, Choosing Stencils, Matching Borders & Corners*, Lafayette, CA: C&T Publishing, 1999.

Montano, Judith Baker. *The Crazy Quilt Handbook, Revised*, 2nd ed., Lafayette, CA: C&T Publishing, 2001.

Quick & Easy Block Tool, Lafayette, CA: C&T Publishing, 2003.

About the AUTHOR

Jennifer Chiaverini, a graduate of the University of Notre Dame and the University of Chicago, taught writing at Pennsylvania State University and Edgewood College before leaving teaching to write full-time. The author of the popular Elm Creek Quilts novels and the first companion book of quilt patterns, *Elm Creek Quilts: Projects Inspired by the Elm Creek Quilts Novels*, Chiaverini is also the designer of the "Elm Creek Quilts" fabric lines from Red Rooster Fabrics. A frequent lecturer at quilt shows and writing conferences, Chiaverini lives in Madison, Wisconsin, with her husband and two young sons.

About the QUILTMAKERS

Laura Blanchard   Gerda's Shoo-Fly, Odd Fellow's Chain

Laura Blanchard has always been interested in quilts. She took her first class in 1987, shortly after moving to Columbus, Ohio, and was instantly hooked. She soon began producing quilts to sell at craft shows. Laura and her family later moved to Virginia, where she began teaching at local quilt shops and guilds. In the six years that she has been teaching, Laura has enjoyed sharing her enthusiasm for quilting and seeing her students' satisfaction in their accomplishments. Laura designs her own patterns and markets them under the name Have2Quilt. She is also a professional designer for Red Rooster Fabrics. Laura and her husband, Ray, live in Midlothian, Virginia. They have two grown children.

Laura Blanchard

Sue Hale   Grace's Friendship block

Sue began making quilts fifteen years ago when she lived in Southern California. Soon, she was working at the Fabric Patch and teaching appliqué classes there and at other area quilt shops. Sue has taught her original designs at the Road to California Quilters' Conference and on a cruise as well. Her appliqué work has appeared in *Quilter's Newsletter Magazine* and in two volumes of Elly Sienkiewicz's Baltimore Beauties series. Since relocating with her husband to Richmond, Virginia, in 1996, Sue has worked as a consultant to Benartex and worked and taught in a quilt shop. Sue is currently a consultant and quilt designer for Red Rooster Fabrics.

Sue Hale

June Pease   Elms and Lilacs

June began her twenty-five-year tenure as a quilter, designer, and teacher in 1978. As an academically trained teacher and enthusiastic quilter, she creates lively, informative classes that appeal to a broad audience. Appliqué and geometric piecework find their way equally in her work. June exhibits and consistently wins ribbons in guilds in New Hampshire and Vermont, including the annual Vermont Quilt Festival. She garnered special recognition at the East Coast Quilter's Alliance—A Quilter's Gathering 2001, where she was awarded the Publisher's Award from *The Quilter Magazine*. Her creations have been offered through the League of New Hampshire Craftsmen and Keepsake Quilting as well as many local craft outlets. June's work has been exhibited at the New England Quilt Museum in Lowell, Massachusetts, and published in *The Quilter Magazine* as well as in *Free-Style Quilts* by Susan Carlson and *Sky Dyes* by Mickey Lawler, both available from C&T Publishing. June is a quilt consultant and designer for Red Rooster Fabrics.

June Pease

Sue Vollbrecht   Wholecloth Crib Quilt

Sue Vollbrecht of Monona, Wisconsin, has been quilting for 28 years. Sue's passion for quiltmaking and background in art led her to teaching, speaking engagements, and quilt pattern design. In 1997, Sue started her longarm quilting business, Quilting Memories, and quickly became known and admired for designing custom patterns to make each customer's quilt unique. Sue lives with her husband Rick, who is very supportive of her quilting endeavors. She is the current treasurer of the Madison, Wisconsin, quilt guild, The Mad City Quilters.

Sue Vollbrecht